The Complete Book
of Home Management

The Complete Book of Home Management

Elva Anson & Kathie Liden

MOODY PRESS

CHICAGO

Library of Congress Cataloging in Publication Data

Anson, Elva.
    The complete book of home management.

    Originally published: The compleat family book.
(Chicago, Ill.): Moody Press, c1979.
    Bibliography: p.
    1. Family life education.   2. Family—Religious
life.   3. Home economics.   I. Liden, Kathie, 1940-
II. Title.
HQ10.A62   1985   646.7′8   84-27180
ISBN 0-8024-1595-4 (pbk.)

8 9 10 11 12 Printing/GB/Year 93 92 91 90 89 88

Printed in the United States of America

Contents

1

How to Achieve Quality Living

If you are somebody's husband or wife and especially if you are also somebody's parent, you probably think that the days fly by and your list of things to do has no end. You may even feel like the pilot who, after a malfunctioning of all the navigational equipment on his plane, said, "I don't know where we're going, but we do have a great tail wind. Wherever we wind up, we should set a new record."

A sense of direction, a plan, can make the difference between responsible family living and just surviving with a group of fellow boarders who happen to be your family. Having a plan gives you control. Add to that organizational skills, sound financing, and healthful eating, and you have the ingredients for vitality and purposeful living.

As Christians we know there is purpose and meaning to life; therefore, it does make a difference what we do and how we act. God has made us stewards of time, talents, resources.

"Let a man regard us in this manner, as servants of Christ, and stewards of the mysteries of God. In this case, moreover, it is

7

required of stewards that one be found trustworthy" (1 Corinthians 4:1-2).

You may feel that you do not know where to start to bring order out of the chaos at your house. Perhaps the thought of making lists and plans completely baffles you.

If you feel overwhelmed by household and family responsibility, you can learn the skills you need to handle it well. It takes determination, but it can be done. Not overnight, but step-by-step as you learn small skills that you can make your very own habits.

Fortunately, you do not have to depend solely on your own power to learn to control time and resources. A Christian marriage includes Someone besides your mate. The third Person is the source of all power, all love, and total wisdom. He is the Creator Himself. He will help you get your priorities straight.

To create time you must give time. It sounds like an even trade, but it is not. It is an investment. Just as money makes money, time makes time.

Time seems to be one thing most American families have little of. In fact, fatigue and time pressure may be the greatest problems facing today's families. We career down the road to old age without taking time to get to know each other. Do not fall for the notion that your busyness is temporary, because that is an illusion. Families pay an enormous price for this kind of life-style.

Several years ago Kathie Liden, coauthor of this book, began researching time management, nutrition, and financial planning. She and her husband, Dave, were looking for ways to help their family have more time and a better quality of life.

It all started when Kathie worked as a volunteer at a children's receiving home. She met children who were underfed, beaten, raped, drugged, and already losers. One evening while Kathie was talking to a Scout leader, she mentioned how much better she communicated with these special children than she did with her own.

"That's easy to understand," he said. "You give your heart, time, and attention to them once a week for two hours."

Kathie began to think about how much time and energy she

had spent planning for Sunday school work, the Children's Receiving Home, and other activities. She thought about how often she put other people first and her family second. She and Dave had many long talks about it. Then they decided to start putting their family first.

In September 1972 they set aside Monday night for their family and called their project Family Council. To prepare, they brushed the dust off the family Bible, listened to tapes, and read everything they could find about Christian families.

The Lidens had begun a new and wonderful adventure. God had become an active member of the family. Communication and love grew by leaps and bounds.

Thousands of families, like the Lidens, are learning the fundamentals for managing their time and their home life to provide the quality of life necessary for nurturing the spirit. We shall explore some of these ideas.

We shall find ways to slow down the family by getting more done in less time. We shall see how to encourage cooperation and independence in the children. We shall take a look at some ideas for putting the family on a sound financial basis. We shall learn what to feed the family to give each member the greatest possible vitality.

CHANGE STARTS WITH YOU

At this point you may be sitting back trying to catch your breath. Perhaps you shake your head and think, *Those ideas may work for some people, but there's no way we can do all that!*

You are right! If you have never taken time to plan, to organize, and to take control of your life, you cannot change overnight. However, you can change one small thing any time you like. Success and growth come from a series of small changes that lead relentlessly toward the goal you have set. The concert pianist has spent hundreds of hours at the piano before he walks on stage. The Olympic medalist learns to swim as a young child.

Studies show that age has little bearing on learning capacity. It is never too late to start. Never too late to change!

First, you must know that you are not happy with things as they are. Then take stock of what it is that you want to change. Talk things over. Determine your priorities. Decide what you want to begin working on first. Not everything, just one small thing.

Face up to your fear of change or fear that it will not work. Clear your mind of negative suggestions. *Refuse* to accept negative thoughts about yourself or what you can do. Replace negative thoughts with positive ones. "Perfect love casts out fear" (1 John 4:18).

Researchers Henry S. Maas and Joseph A. Kuypers of the University of California at Berkeley studied the lives of 142 men and women over a forty-year period. They found that those who were active and happy when they were younger remained active and happy as they aged. The group that was depressed, anxious, or bored, had felt that way and had had the same problems when they were forty years younger.

"The answer," notes Kuypers, "lies in preserving the capability to play, to be experimental with yourself. The key is flexibility—in the way you work, deal with family and friends—in all spheres of life."[1]

Flexibility means the willingness to grow and change. Can you become an organized person if you have been unorganized all your life? Can you learn to communicate with members of your family? Can you learn how to establish family activities and meetings? Can you change your family's diet if you need to? Can you work systematically to control your finances? The answer to all these questions is, "Yes! If you really want to!"

The fact that you are reading this book shows a positive attitude. That positive attitude makes it possible for you to accept the challenge created by change and to grow as a Christian. You can choose change, defy your fears, and take that first step necessary to act on your decisions.

When you commit yourself fully to a new way of doing things, when you take that first step, you bring your total being into that action—your past experiences, your abilities, your undeveloped potential. By doing this you make it possible for God to make you the person He intended. He brings out strengths you did not even know you had. You will continually surprise yourself and live in a state of exhilaration and discovery. This is what growing is all about.

God makes you a new creature when you are willing to commit yourself in faith to new ways of doing things. Most of us use only one-tenth of the power to act that God has given us. By committing ourselves to a new course of action we begin drawing on the other ninety percent. You can achieve anything that God puts in your mind as a goal.

You can say with Paul, "I do not regard myself as having laid hold of it yet; but one thing I do: forgetting what lies behind and reaching forward to what lies ahead, I press on toward the goal for the prize of the upward call of God in Christ Jesus" (Philippians 3:13-14).

FOCUS ON YOUR DIVINE PARTNER

Every husband makes both positive and negative contributions to his wife, and every wife makes positive and negative contributions to her husband. Too often we focus on the negative contributions. But when our eyes and minds direct our attention to negative actions, we spend all our creative energy getting nowhere. Involving ourselves in problems paralyzes action and makes it impossible for us to find solutions.

Over and over the Bible instructs us to focus on the most important member of our partnership, Jesus Christ. When we fill our minds with Him and His power, change and growth can take place.

Colossians 2:10 tells us: "And in Him you have been made complete, and He is the head over all rule and authority."

2 Corinthians 3:5 says: "Not that we are adequate in ourselves to consider anything as coming from ourselves, but our adequacy is from God."

It is a matter of priority. By keeping God first in our families, other things fall into place.

Jesus told us in Matthew 6:33: "But seek first His kingdom and His righteousness; and all these things shall be added to you."

The great King Eternal, the Creator of the universe, wants to be your partner. He wants you to succeed. What is more, He promises His power and His strength.

Suppose someone deposits $1 million dollars in your bank account. If you do not believe it is there, or if you forget about it, it will do you no good. But any time you write a check or withdraw from the account, you can have whatever you want.

God has deposited in each of our accounts an unmeasurable amount of power so that we may do what God wants. All we have to do is draw on it.

In Romans 8:37 Paul tells us that in all things we overwhelmingly conquer through Him who loved us. Ephesians 3:20 says: "Now to Him who is able to do exceeding abundantly beyond all that we ask or think, according to the power that works within us."

Our dependence is on God. It is through His power that we can do all things. Jesus modeled for us the method for drawing on God's power.

Mark 1:35 says: "And in the early morning, while it was still dark, He arose and went out and departed to a lonely place, and was praying there."

Throughout His ministry Jesus sought God's instructions through prayer. We, too, can find our sense of direction, our motivation for action, and the strength we need to act, through prayer.

Who, then, can be successful? The person, loved by God, who seeks God's will and knows that he can do anything God wants him to do, if he wants to do it badly enough. A winner, like Paul, says, "I can! I will!" He does not say, "I wish I could but I can't because . . ."

You have to be patient and tenacious. You have to have faith in yourself and in God. You must act on the power that is yours for the taking. Proverbs 16:3 says:

> Commit your works to the LORD
> And your plans will be established.

You will not be discouraged and frustrated if your plans are "established," and you know that you are doing what God wants. You can act in faith, knowing that each step you take—and each day you live—is bringing you closer to ultimate fulfillment—finishing the work God gave you to do.

GROWING AND CHANGING

When Everett and I first married, we argued about whether our intense love for each other could last.

"Be practical," he told me. "Look at people who have been married a long time. They don't love each other like this. We have to expect things to change as we grow older."

"Our love should grow," I would answer. "I can't imagine loving each other less."

Do people change, and if so, is change desirable? Do you want your spouse always to be just the way he or she was on your wedding day?

Let us face it. Change is inevitable. In fact, marriage involves a series of changes. The birth of a baby. Buying a house. Moving. Going back to school or work. Losing a job. Going into business for yourself. Sickness. Economic changes. Reading a book like this and deciding to become more organized or to make diet changes. The list goes on and on.

Everett was right about change, but after twenty-three years of marriage he happily admits that the change has been positive, not negative. Change involves giving up some behavior or attitude that has been important to you in the past. Change involves risk. You know what will happen if you behave in the old way; but how will you—and other people—react if you change?

Do you remember when Jesus told Peter to push the boat farther out in the water and let down his nets for a catch? Peter could have responded in a number of ways, but he took the risk of doing what Jesus said. As a result he caught more fish than he ever imagined could be caught.

On another occasion Jesus told Peter to come to Him while He was walking on the water. Peter got out of the boat and became the only man in history—other than Jesus Himself—to walk on the surface of a body of water. Again, Peter had taken a risk. As long as he kept his eyes on Jesus, all went well. When he looked around at the wind-blown waves, he began to sink.

Desire to change must be joined with willingness to take risk. As in Peter's case, fear will make change impossible. 2 Timothy 1:7 says: "For God has not given us a spirit of timidity, but of power and love and discipline."

When we consider change we often hesitate, afraid to take the first step. It is not enough to decide to become better organized or to make marriage a working partnership. We must act on that decision. Until we act on our decisions, they are only wishes.

When we do commit ourselves fully to a course of action, when we take the first step, we bring our total selves into it. More often than not we must also discard attitudes and habits. We must give up regrets about the past, fears of the future, and false concepts of ourselves and our spouses, such as feeling unworthy or incapable. We must clear the negative thoughts from our minds and replace them with positive thoughts.

"I *can* do all things through Christ which strengtheneth me" (Philippians 4:13, KJV,* italics added).

I can! I can! I can!

Sometimes change begins as you discover yourself in a new relationship with your partner. If your attitudes change, the same mate, the same house, and the same job can seem fresh and new. The steps you take to rebuild on the same ground may be small, and change will be gradual. You may go two steps forward and one step back.

Do not become discouraged. Change can be more meaningful when you have a chance to experience the old way with the new. The important thing is not to try to move forward by trying to

*King James Version.

leap three or four steps at once. Falling that far could be so discouraging that you would never want to move forward again.

Several years ago the United States Small Business Administration funded a number of tests to see how much achievement motivation was had by people with plans to operate small businesses. The experimenters set up a spike at one end of a room in a downtown Baltimore office building. They gave each participant a handful of rope rings to pitch onto the spike.

There was no fixed line to toss from. Some people stood quite close, easily ringing the spike—and quickly lost interest. Others stood relatively far away, failed to make any ringers, and became discouraged. A few stood just far enough away to make the toss challenging, yet not so far as to make success impossible. These were the successful players.

If you want your home life to improve, look for the half-steps that lead to the change you want to make. Each step should be challenging but definitely within your reach. To take even a half-step, you must commit yourself to an investment of time. When you have made that commitment, you are on your way.

CONFIDENT EXPECTATION

Is it not amazing how often man thinks he has made a new discovery, whereas the Bible gave us that truth long before present-day scientists "discovered" it? Through experiments, Harvard psychologist David McClelland discovered that by changing the ways people thought about themselves and their surroundings, he could change their actual performance.[2] Once an individual's fantasies and thoughts are programmed, his subconscious can urge him on instead of blocking him.

The Bible tells us in Proverbs 23:7 that as a man thinks in his heart, so is he. Think about the things you want to experience. If you want to change something in your life, you must change your thoughts and keep them changed.

Visualize success. If you want to become better organized, for example, picture yourself as an organized person. Let your mind dwell on the advantage of being better organized rather than on how difficult it will be. Create a strong, clear mental picture. You will find what you have visualized gradually happening as you begin taking small steps in that direction.

Jesus said that all things are possible to him that believes. (Mark 9:23).

Lack of belief in your ability to reach your goal can cause you to fail. That is why you must train your mind by first taking small steps that you know you can accomplish. Your abilities and talents will grow as you use them.

Remember the power of the tongue. James compares the tongue to the bit we put in the horse's mouth in order to make him obey us and to the very small rudder of a ship that enables its pilot to make it go where he wants it to go. Whatever a man continually says, he will begin to turn into reality.

Those who constantly talk about how unorganized they are will continue to be unorganized. By talking about negative characteristics, you give them more attention than they deserve and increase their power. At the same time you block the finer qualities you want to develop. You can deliberately choose which of your qualities you want to express.

The subconscious mind does not recognize good or bad any more than the soil recognizes the difference in the seed planted. Whatever seed you put in the soil is the one that grows. In the same way, whatever thoughts you put into your subconscious determine what you become. You sow words and thoughts. You will reap what you sow.

Instead of wasting energy worrying about how your efforts will turn out, concentrate on what you are doing at the moment. Live one day at a time; take one step at a time.

Harvard psychologist William James said, "The greatest discovery of my lifetime is that a man can change the circumstances of his life by changing his thoughts and his attitudes."

As long as you hang on to negative beliefs about yourself, you cannot change. Change comes from within. The potential is there to become the organized person you ought to be. It is up to you to act out that belief with the power God has put in your account.

Become aware of the power of your thoughts. Whenever you do anything at all—think, speak, or act—something happens as a result. Make this law work for your benefit by choosing your thoughts and actions carefully.

Continually practice confident expectation.

SUCCESS BREEDS SUCCESS

It may be helpful to have each member of the family write down all the good qualities he knows he has. You may include incidents when you felt you achieved success. Help each other by adding to the lists. By listing your assets you create a foundation on which to build success.

By focusing on what you have done successfully in the past, you can repeat what works for you and perhaps add a little to it. Succeeding gives you a feeling of confidence and the courage to do something more.

For example, a child who has learned to read at the primary level has no trouble going on, one step at a time, to more challenging reading. His past success gives him the courage and motivation to read more. The payoff is an increase in the number of reading choices he has.

Establish a success pattern. When you decide on the first step toward a goal, start with something you know you can do. Be sure you do what you set out to do. You cannot expect your subconscious to pay attention to you if you do not follow through.

Now build on the success of your first step. The next step will be the next easiest, and so on until you have established a success pattern.

If your relationship with your spouse or a son or daughter has deteriorated, concentrate on the happy times you had together. Love is the most powerful force on earth; God is love. If hate and resentment come into your mind, immediately replace them with thoughts of love and of happy times. Continually pray for the one you wish to love.

A Christian should be a channel through which God's love flows, but love cannot flow through a clogged channel. Are resentments and hate blocking the flow of God's love through you? Ask for God's forgiveness and forgive yourself. Forgiveness sets you free to love again.

Freedom to love also gives you freedom to change. Love casts out fear and gives you courage to risk moving forward step by step.

DEFEAT DOES NOT MEAN FAILURE

Booker T. Washington said, "Success is to be measured not so much by the position that one has reached in life as by the obstacles which he has overcome while trying to succeed."

By taking two steps forward and one step back, we still continually move closer to the goal. A man who makes no mistakes is one who does nothing. Failure, disappointments, and setbacks are a part of life. We must learn not to identify with our failures.

Before Thomas Edison succeeded in inventing the light bulb, he failed two thousand times. He saw each failure as a part of ultimate success. He knew that each time he discovered something that would not work, he was closer to discovering what would work.

There are many many examples of people who overcame backward steps. Abraham Lincoln ran for political office seven times and was defeated each time. Bobby Kennedy failed third grade and could not even take care of his own paper route. Babe Ruth struck out more times than any other baseball player. Ed Gibson, one of the astronauts on the Skylab III mission, failed first and fourth grades.

Learn from your mistakes, but identify with your success. Press on, confident in your own ability to succeed backed by the power of God. Never forget that people who accomplish great things believe they can do it.

You can be like the timid swimmer who, upon seeing a large wave, panics and runs, only to be caught, knocked to the sand, and immersed in the cold rushing water. Or you can be like the surfer who looks for the giant wave, prepares to meet it, rises above it, and is carried far.

THE PAYOFF

Once you begin to achieve quality living, the rewards, both direct and indirect, far outnumber the risks. The atmosphere in your home will change. You will recognize a new spirit of cooperation and caring.

Orderliness and stability will result from an organized approach to running the house. This will bring shorter hours of housework, more time for leisure, and thus more time with each other. This increases your freedom to do the things you really want to do, including the many things you may always have wanted to do for friends and neighbors and to promote the work of the church. It also increases your freedom to grow as individuals.

Setting goals in finances and time management will give you a sense of direction. You will feel in control, with God's help. This will make available more money and more time to give what you really want to life. You will not be drifting aimlessly, helplessly reacting to whatever happens to you.

By knowledgeably providing good food for your family, you will supply each member with the energy he needs to get things done. You will have peace of mind, knowing that you are providing the best nourishment available at the lowest possible cost.

By training your children to be independent physically, financially, and spiritually, you give them the confidence to succeed in their own marriages or other future commitments.

Best of all family members will have a feeling of worth and belonging as they continually commit themselves to each other and to their divine partner Jesus Christ. You will know that you are being a good steward for the One to whom you are ultimately accountable. You can look forward to His "Well done, My son/daughter."

2

Management Begins at Home

WORK AS A TEAM

The Bible teaches us to live together in harmony, to live together in love as though we had only one mind and one spirit among us (Philippians 2:2). Living together in harmony and love forms the foundation on which we build the marriage relationship. It is the key to our attitudes, the way we raise our children, who does what, how we operate this partnership, how we manage our finances, how we take care of our bodies, and how we cope with change.

Joe, a man who had not learned to unclutter his life, could never find anything when he wanted it. One of Joe's co-workers grew so tired of helping him keep track of his tools that he told him in disgust, "You need a rent a mom!"

For years Joe's wife, Bonnie, had struggled with the same problem. She did not want to mother him, but she did not know how to help.

"Joe is a brilliant man and a loving husband," she said, "but he could never find his glasses, his hammer, or the car keys. Not until the guy at work suggested he needed to 'rent a mom,' did he admit he had a problem."

You cannot rent a mom. A woman who feels like one usually is

21

not happy about it. A spirit of cooperation must exist in your marriage, and each person must carry part of the load. When partners pool their resources and develop team spirit, they mutually benefit.

Ray and Charlotte have a beautiful partnership. "Ray and I have been through rough years when we were both ready to give up and call it quits," says Charlotte. "I guess that's why we appreciate the strong relationship we have now and care deeply about each other's feelings and needs. We enjoy our kids very much, but we're also looking forward to the day when it's just the two of us."

"When our kids were little, I liked to bathe them every night," Ray says, "because it gave Charlotte more time to spend with me. At the same time it gave me an excuse to be with the kids. I have always had a hard time expressing myself, and I might never have gotten acquainted with the children if I hadn't spent that time with them."

Ray still takes time to be with his children one at a time. In this way he can find out what their needs are and show them how much he cares about them.

In this family everyone has responsibility. Mike empties the trash, cleans the pool, and helps Ray with the yard work. Since he does not go to school until eleven o'clock, he sometimes helps his mother by emptying the dishwasher or running the vacuum.

Judi and Shawn take turns setting and clearing the table and washing the dishes. Both girls help with the housework. All three children must keep their own rooms clean, and strip and make their own beds.

"If we're having company or want to go somewhere, everyone pitches in and gets done whatever has to be done," Charlotte says. "Ray has no hang-up about helping in the house. It does not threaten his masculinity. He's always willing to help—not if I'm sitting in a chair reading a book, of course—but if I really need help."

"We have learned to value our time together as a family," says

Ray, "because the kids are growing up so fast. We love them dearly, but we also value our time together as a couple. When our kids are grown, I don't want to look at Charlotte and say, 'Who are you?' "

Ray and Charlotte have found a workable solution to who does what. Unfortunately, you cannot copy their solution. Because you are unique people, you must assess your own needs, abilities, and desires and come up with your own solution.

There are no specific rules for how a house must be run and no standards by which to measure success. You must choose whatever housekeeping style suits your family and meets its needs best. This will be different for different periods of your lives.

Do not make the mistake of measuring housecleaning by someone else's standards. To keep things in perspective, remember that if it will not matter ten years from now, do not worry about it.

As a team you will learn to distinguish between your wants and your needs. What one of you wants may be irrelevant in terms of the needs of the other or of the marriage itself. Sometimes one partner's needs are more urgent than the other's at that moment. You must learn to make that kind of judgment. Most of the time you can find solutions that meet the needs of everyone.

When we first married, for example, Everett was going to college, and I was teaching school. We decided that Everett needed to study during the afternoons and evenings. I had to find something to do to occupy myself and stay out of his way during those times. Saturday mornings we did the housework together. The rest of the weekend was ours to spend as we pleased. We usually spent the entire weekend together—a delightful time for us both.

From the beginning of their marriage Dave and Kathie used their time and abilities to learn the skills necessary to build their home life. Dave would take a class to help his career as a surveyor. On the same night Kathie would take a class on money management. The second year Dave added more business classes while Kathie took interior decorating and real estate. Later, they both took classes on food and time management. They pooled their knowledge and became a fantastic team.

Instead of spending an entire evening watching television, Kathie and Dave spent at least an hour five or six days a week talking to each other about the day. Then they share portions of books they are reading. They learn twice as much as they could individually, and they have confidence in big decisions each may make that will affect the family.

The Lidens specialize in buying old houses and fixing them up to sell. "When Dave comes home, and I tell him I sold the house today, he trusts my judgment and knows I can handle such a transaction," Kathie says.

Cooperation is the key to this kind of teamwork. It keeps a marriage running smoothly and lifts it over the tough spots. If you set up your marriage as a contest instead of a partnership, nobody wins. Work out disagreements in a spirit of harmony and work as a team managing your home and family.

The two of you need to plan your future. Visualize your lives five years from now. What do you hope to be doing in family living, employment, finances, recreation? What kind of spiritual growth can you expect? What skills must you develop to achieve your goals? What kind of self-improvement program do you need?

What obstacles keep you from becoming what you want to be? How can you get rid of these obstacles? Focus your attention on your objectives rather than on the obstacles, if you wish to succeed. When you discover alternative paths to your objectives, using resources in new ways, you will break your old habits and change your life.

INVOLVE THE WHOLE FAMILY

Bring the family members together. Ask them to start dreaming and thinking with you about specific areas concerning the family. What do they want to accomplish? Set up a specific family time on a regular basis. This will provide an opportunity for the whole family to participate—to settle grievances, to make family decisions, to have fun.

People who know the Lawson family marvel at how smoothly things go for parents Don and Loretta and their four children, who range in age from toddler to early teen.

"We have been having family night every week for about four years," Loretta says. "We take turns presiding and planning activities. We have a lot of fun together. At our family meetings we also set up work charts and establish family rules. We seldom have any problem getting cooperation from the children, because they know they help run the home."

If you have never had family night, how do you begin? There are many ways to begin, but here is one suggestion. Sit around a table or in some other kind of circular arrangement so everyone can see everyone else. Always start the evening with prayer. Father will explain what family night will be. He will let the children know that from now on one night or afternoon a week will be set aside just for the family. He will tell them you expect to play together, sing together, go places together, talk over problems, talk about God, and just enjoy being together and getting to know each other better.

Have a notebook handy. Ask questions. Find out what your family would like to talk about and have fun doing. A few minutes of brainstorming can produce volumes of ideas. One family spent an hour the first night and filled four sheets of paper with ideas.

Here are just a few of many ideas you might consider: makeup night (put mustaches and makeup on parents' faces), pass around a feeling bag (put an object in a bag, and each one tries to guess what it is by feeling it), make a collage on love, make treasure boxes for items family members collect, have a banquet night, make sailboats and sail them, make kites and fly them, play games, work on puzzles, tell stories, write and put on plays, write or read riddle and joke books, make puppets and put on puppet shows, show family home movies and slides, have celebrations and family parties, go on picnics, model clay, exercise, bicycle, skate, walk, do role playing, visit factories, visit a farm, have a fix-it night.

Have a love night for Grandma. Make her cookies or write letters to her. Learn a foreign language, have discussions and debates, plan and plant a garden, make terrariums, have a fire drill, take an imaginary journey, write letters, make valentines, cook or bake, make candles or shrink art, carve soap.

On the first few nights plan activities and refreshments that you know will be well received. It is like opening a new business. You want your customers to have a good first impression.

During one of the first family nights, you might talk about the purpose of families. This is a good time to tell the children how you met, fell in love, and married. Dig out an old album and show them pictures of those years. Talk about your first date, impressions, and joys. Tell each one about his birth and how happy you felt when he arrived and how much you still love him.

Have everyone list what he thinks families should be. What do you expect from your family? Focus on each person, one at a time. What do you know about that person? What is his favorite color? What does he like to do best? Who is his best friend? What kind of people does he like? How do you think his friends see him? What is his favorite Bible verse? Let everyone write answers to these questions. Then have the subject give the true answers.

End the evening with prayer, refreshments, and some plans for the following week. You might draw names for prayer partners during the week. On the next family night you will reveal whose name you had.

The length of your family meeting will vary according to the age of the children. All meetings should end before the children get bored or restless. You should know what you can reasonably expect of a child at any given age and thus avoid expecting too much or too little of him. If your children are very young, fifteen minutes may be all the time you can expect them to spend on family night.

In a family with a wide range in ages, there will be times when the older children and the parents need to talk about or do something with which the little children cannot relate. At these times, spend a short time with the younger ones, who then can play by themselves until refreshment time. Use common sense in adapting plans to the needs of your family.

To make family night work, you must be prepared. Can you imagine the president of a large corporation coming to a staff meeting unprepared? Neither should parents gather a family together for a meeting when they have no idea what they plan to do. If you ask your family, "What shall we do tonight?" you will get as many answers as there are members of the family. Conflict and chaos result.

About three times a year Everett and I take a weekend to do nothing but relax and consider the direction we want our family to take. We leave the children at home and find a place where we can hide away for a day or two. We take stacks of material and blank calendars.

We come home with tentative plans for the next two or three months. The calendar for the current month goes up on our kitchen bulletin board where the children can see what we plan to do. I check the calendar each week to see what materials we need so we shall never be caught without them.

Kathie and Dave plan this way also. If they cannot get away for the weekend, they spend a Saturday morning in the park, reviewing and planning. Sometimes these plans change. That is fine. Plans can be broken. Flexibility is the key.

Book stores now offer an abundance of material to help with family-night plans. Here are some books that are helpful:

Anson, Elva. *How to Keep the Family That Prays Together from Falling Apart*. Chicago: Moody, 1975.

Baumann, Clayton, comp., and Merrill, Dean, ed. *125 Crowd Breakers*. Glendale, Calif.: Regal, 1974.

Bock, Lois, and Working, Mijo. *Happiness Is a Family Time Together*. Old Tappan, N.J.: Revell, 1975.

Duckert, Mary. *Intergenerational Experiences in Church Education*. Philadelphia: JED Geneva, 1976.

Gospel Light Publications. *Family Life Today* (A monthly periodical). Box 1591, Glendale, Calif. 91209.

Griggs, Donald, and Griggs, Patricia. *Generations Learning Together.* Livermore, Calif: Griggs Educational Service, 1976.

Lessor, Richard. *Fuzzies.* Chicago: Argus Communications, 1971.

Rickerson, Wayne E. *Getting Your Family Together.* Glendale, Calif.: Regal, 1977.

Rogers, Sharee, and Rogers, Jack. *The Family Together* (Intergenerational education in the church school). Los Angeles: Action House, 1976.

Satir, Virginia. *Conjoint Family Therapy.* Palo Alto, Calif.: Science and Behavior, 1967.

————. *Peoplemaking.* Palo Alto, Calif.: Science and Behavior, 1972.

Walker, Georgianna, ed. *The Celebration Book.* Glendale, Calif.: Regal, 1977.

Waschow, Louise. *Experiential Exercise for Family Clusters* (mimeographed exercises). 73 Montford Avenue, Mill Valley, Calif. 94941.

PRINCIPLES OF MANAGEMENT

A man and woman who manage their household well, whether they know it or not, apply techniques necessary for running any organization smoothly. Let us take a look at some of these techniques.

PLANNING

You will need to take a look at what is going on and plan for the future. Everyone in the family should be informed of plans so that each one has a sense of direction.

ORGANIZATION

The house, people, equipment, and finances must be organized in a way that will make possible the family's easily reaching the goals and objectives they have set.

AUTHORITY

Someone must be in charge. He must set a good example,

bring the members of the family together, and make sure there is unity of direction.

HARMONY

"Live together in harmony, live together in love, as though you had only one mind and one spirit between you" (Philippians 2:2, Phillips*).

DECISIONS

Before you make a decision, analyze your motives. Ask yourself, What is the best choice for the family? When you make the decision, state it clearly and precisely so no one in the family misunderstands what you have decided.

JOB CLIMATE

Treat each member of the family with fairness and respect. Encourage everyone to be creative. Value initiative and responsibility so that family members will value these characteristics also. Praise and reward those who do a job well. Continual affirmation of each other will do much to insure the success of the family.

CONTROL

Control requires evaluation to see that the family stays on the right track. It involves periodic consultations among members of the family so that everyone has an opportunity to contribute his ideas or complaints. It may mean modifying plans or changing ways of doing things if they sidetrack the family from reaching clearly stated goals. As long as there is control, the family will stay headed in the direction you want it to go.

ATTITUDE CHECK

You may want to establish a method to quickly check up on attitudes. High school youngsters at our church have discovered an effective method for doing this. When tempers become a little short or activities bog down, someone calls out, "Attitude check!" Immediately everyone mentally runs down an attitude list. If he can align himself on the positive side of the list, he calls out, "Praise the Lord." If he cannot, he realizes that the prob-

*J. B. Phillips, The New Testament in Modern English.

lems experienced may stem from his own negative attitude.

A family also might use this method. Here is a suggested checklist:

1. Acceptance or rejection
2. Adaptable or rigid
3. Admiration or ridicule
4. Cooperation or competition
5. Courage or fear
6. Faith or doubt
7. Forgive or hold grudges
8. Organized or sloppy

Your family may add to this list. Post the list on the family bulletin board. Starting at the top, designate "Acceptance or rejection" as the attitude of the day. Copy it on cards and put up the cards all over the house. This will give the family visual reminders of the attitude you want to strive for on that particular day. The following day move on to number two, and so on down the list.

By emphasizing positive attitudes, we make ourselves attitude conscious, and that will certainly go a long way toward improving the effectiveness of family living.

How You Dress Does Make a Difference

What does dress have to do with management? Probably much more than you realize. Imagine for a minute that you walked into your classroom and found the teacher at his desk but dressed in pajamas. Or you entered a department store and found the clerk dressed in overalls and her hair in curlers. Or when you visited the doctor's office, you found him waiting for you, barefoot, shirtless, and in gym shorts.

Ridiculous? Of course, but it illustrates the point that how you dress does make a difference. Most people believe this is true until they walk through the front doors of their homes. Then that truth becomes invalid for them, and when it comes to dress, anything goes. Actually, the truth does not change. How you dress affects the way you manage your home.

Parents struggle morning after morning with the problem of getting Junior off to the school bus on time as he looks for a missing sock or shoe. Women in nightgowns and lounging robes sluggishly try to do their housework and wonder why they barely get the breakfast dishes done before it is time for the morning coffee break. Father sits in front of the television, Coke in hand, clad only in cutoffs, as an unrestricted, sagging, hairy stomach blurs out the place where his belt should be, and wonders why sons can be so stubborn about their sloppy clothes. Dress plays a part in all these problems.

If you teach Junior to get up and get dressed before he comes to breakfast, he will not be looking for that elusive shoe and sock when the bus drives up. If a woman dresses in practical, attractive, comfortable clothes, she may discover new energy that will help her do her work in a businesslike way because she is dressed for work and not for lounging. The father who does not sit around the house like a slob stands a greater chance of keeping his son's respect. He also has a leg to stand on when he discusses with his children differences of opinion about dress.

Have you ever stopped to think about various jobs and how differently people dress for them? Nurses, for example, wear white uniforms, because such clothes are uniquely appropriate for the care of sick people. Analyze the activity you plan to do and dress accordingly. A nightgown and lounging robe are great when you want to relax and go to sleep, but they certainly are not conducive to energetic housecleaning.

Simplify the wardrobes of family members. The less you have hanging in the closet, the less you have to take care of. Most people wear ten to twenty percent of their total wardrobe eighty percent of the time. Experts suggest nine wearable outfits as adequate. If you have twelve, you will have three extra outfits for special occasions. A few outfits, all in good condition, keep you better dressed than a closetful of clothes that have not been carefully chosen.

Thoughtfully plan each person's wardrobe. To do this, have

everyone write down all his activities during the past two weeks and what he wore. Be sure to include activities at home. Add some typical, though not regular, activities and how you usually dress for them. This will give you an accurate idea of what kinds of activities make up your life-style.

Next, take an inventory of what you have. You will have to set aside a few hours for this job. Our family spent one family night going through closets. As you go through yours, decide whether your clothes fit your needs.

Your wardrobe should reflect your life-style. Clothes for your main activities should dominate your wardrobe. To plan for the special activities, buy clothes that are versatile. Mix-and-match items will make your clothes versatile. Always coordinate your entire wardrobe.

Try on each garment and see if it fits your goal. Is it comfortable? Does it go well with the other clothes in your closet? Does it make you feel good? Will it make you more effective in the performance of your activity? Does it enhance your physical characteristics, make you more attractive? Is it easy to care for?

Remember, when your teenager goes through his wardrobe, *he* decides if his clothes make him feel good. The question is not Do his clothes make his parents feel good? The parent who insists on dictating one style while all the other kids wear another style may unknowingly alienate the youngster from the group. At a time when the child becomes concerned about changing body proportions, you do not want to make him feel that he is different from the others of similar age. Give him guidance, but do not try to impose your adult tastes if it is just a question of style.

You will need to separate your clothes into three piles: those you want to keep, those you want to discard, and those that can be altered or repaired. Put the clothes to be repaired in your sewing center for attention as soon as possible. Now you will have to decide what you must add to your wardrobe within the limit of your budget.

Again, consider the family as a whole. Whose needs are most

urgent? It might help to make up a clothing list, assigning priorities to the items on it.

Do not ever forget that your heavenly Partner cares very much about how you look and dress. He loved beauty so much that He created a vast variety of multicolored birds, fish, and flowers, and scenery so awesomely beautiful the human mind can scarcely absorb the wonder of it.

It is this God who gave the Israelites detailed instructions for building a beautiful Ark and tabernacle, and who also tells us we are temples of the Holy Spirit. Does it seem right for us to expect the Holy Spirit to live in a temple we have neglected?

God tells us, "Whether, then, you eat or drink or whatever you do, do all to the glory of God" (1 Corinthians 10:31).

How you dress does make a difference. What do your clothes say about you?

DEDICATE YOUR HOME AND FAMILY TO GOD

One day some friends invited us to the blessing of their home and family. They had invited a few Christian friends and their pastor to share in their joy over establishing a new home. In the presence of their friends they dedicated their new dwelling and the family that would occupy it to God and asked His blessing on them.

Since then I have heard about many families who have done something similar. When they move into a new home, they stop to ask God's blessing on it and on them as a family. Some make this a family celebration in which members of the family unite to ask God to bless their new home. Others invite friends and make it a grand occasion in which many people witness the commitment of their home to God. One family asked their pastor to celebrate the Lord's Supper in their home, and friends shared in the Communion service.

However you do it, dedicate your home to God. And never forget that He will live there too, the silent but most powerful member of your family.

3

The House You Live In

TURN YOUR HOUSE INTO A HOME

Ideally, a marital partnership exists in a *home*, not just in a building with four walls and a roof. A house, apartment, or duplex is nothing more than a structure enclosing space. You must turn this space you have rented, leased, or bought into a home.

Make it a place where you can find peace, warmth, excitement, and a lift for your spirits. You want your home to say something about you—what you do, what you like, and what you value. It should facilitate reaching goals you have set for yourself and the marriage. It should be as functional as you can make it.

A home reflects the personalities of those who live in it. "We shape our houses then our houses shape us," said Winston Churchill. Not only does your home reflect who you are, it also affects who you are. So it is important to put a lot of thought and care into turning your house into a home.

What you like may be the first thing you will have to find out. Many of us simply do not know. How do we find out what we like and whether or not our tastes agree with our spouse's?

35

Kathie and Dave made up a questionnaire to get some idea of what each of them liked. They titled it "My Dream House." Here is the questionnaire as Kathy filled it out:

My Dream House

Name: Kathie Liden

Personality type: Bright spring. I like adventure, variety, and change. I dislike being stuck with something forever unless it is my favorite accessory. I like to create whimsical pictures made from patchwork fabrics, do oil paintings on wood, tin, or canvas. I like to make my own curtains, patchwork quilts, and have visual inspirational quotes and poems around me. I want a cheerful atmosphere that says, "Welcome home, family," and, to friends, "Relax, enjoy yourselves, pull up a chair, and stay awhile." Above all, I want my house insulated with Christ and joy!

Style of home: Colonial, country-house feeling. Informal and lots of windows. I want it to have a feeling of happy, fun-loving Christians living within. I want it to have a light, sunny, fresh look.

My favorite things:

Fruit, flowers, vegetables: daisies, daffodils in wicker baskets, bright red geraniums in clay pots, apples in wooden bowls, strawberries painted on wood or appliqued on fabric (cute, mischievous, whimsical—not serious).

Fabrics and designs: crisp white, Wedgewood blue cottons; windowpane plaids; checks and calico prints; small flower prints; polka dots; eyelet; applique; cross-stitch; quilting; scallops; ruffles; ball fringe and rickrack.

Furniture: light pine furniture (old pie safes, harvest tables, rolltop desk), wicker, antiques with old-fashioned accents, trunks with calico linings, painted furniture (some with tole painting), turned legs and posts, spindles, brass beds (dust ruffles and pillow shams).

Windows and walls: tieback curtains, painted and natural shutters, scalloped shades, stained glass, stenciled walls, white walls and paneling, wallpaper (sometimes on the kitchen ceiling, too!), old-fashioned plate rail for collection of pewter and blue and white dishes, beam ceilings.

Floors: brick, pinewood floors, braided rugs and smooth carpet (not deep shag), candy-stripe carpet.

Accessories: handmade quilts, baskets (some for clutter, some for flowers or bulbs; the inside of some quilted for handwork), ruffled patchwork or applique pillows, ferns and ivy, old wooden boxes with straw flowers, eggs in straw, primitive and hand-painted art work (mostly what I do myself), butter churn and old kitchen tools, old clocks, family photos in the hall, poems and quotes to remind me of Christ, family, friends, and fun.

Color: pastels, red, white, blue, yellow, and green.

Dave's responses were not much different from Kathie's, but he liked dark heavy pine, leather, and so on. You can give the questionnaire to teenaged children as well. A house can reflect several personalities. Children's rooms should uniquely reflect their own interests and tastes.

Use a questionnaire, this one or one you make up, as a springboard for discussion. Talk about what you like and do not like. What kinds of things do you like to do? How would you like to live? Do you have hobbies that can go into the decorating? Are you a do-it-yourselfer? Knowing what you like is all a part of communication, goals, life-style.

PLAN CAREFULLY

Visit furniture stores. Go through model homes. When you visit friends, notice their furnishings. Tell each other what you liked and what you did not like.

Go through magazines and books. Clip things you like from the magazines. You may mount them on paper and file them in a binder that you have divided into sections labeled according to rooms. Include store names, prices, fabric samples, and any other information that will be useful.

Eventually, you will find general patterns to your taste. You will know if you like things simple or fancy, contemporary or traditional, colorful or subdued. You will see where you are together and where you are apart.

Do not rush. Take your time and be patient. Making a home is a life-long task. You must make the most of what you have. Good taste is not a matter of money. Pleasant surroundings depend more on careful selection than on money spent.

Once you know what you want, you must decide what you need and can afford. Have a plan that includes a budget and a timetable to guide you in stages to your goal. If you overspend, no matter how attractive your home looks, you cannot live comfortably in it. Learn to live with the money, time, and talent you have available to you *today*—and *plan for tomorrow*.

Make a checklist of basic home furnishings. Check what you have, what you need, and what you can do without. Developing a plan and cutting costs will challenge your ingenuity. Perhaps you can pick up some pieces at a garage sale or from a relative. Resist the temptation to bring home something whether you like it or not, simply because you can get it free. Repair, cover, or paint used furniture to fit the style of your home.

Do not spend all your money on one or two items. You can stretch limited funds farther by buying basics, such as shelving boards, shelf brackets, paint, and a few basic tools. A shelf can serve as a desk, eating area, storage place, or decorative addition. You might make all four for what it would cost to purchase one desk, kitchen table, or set of bookshelves.

TIPS ON DECORATING

SELECT ONE ROOM AT A TIME TO DECORATE

Collect fifteen to twenty pictures of the type of room, furniture, and ideas you like. Tack them up on a bulletin board. Studying these will help you decide just why you like a certain item. Choose your favorite color, texture, and pattern for the room. Paint and carpet change the appearance of rooms more than any other item.

Store your pictures in file folders and place in a dishpan. File under bathroom, kitchen, and so on. A standard notebook is an extra help for storing ideas from magazines and written material. In your notebook keep a section titled "Present Home." When you paint or buy wallpaper, record the amount, brand, and where purchased. Write down how much wallpaper and paint each room took and keep a wallpaper sample clipped to your notebook for color comparison when making repairs.

On graph paper draw the dimensions of your room, scaled ¼ or ½ inch to a foot. Mark the location of all windows and doors. Locate light switches and wall plugs. Draw or use purchased cutouts of furniture that correspond with the floor plan scale. Move the cutouts around until you have the furniture arrangement that pleases you. You may want to color the cutouts to balance the color scheme.

Lay a large piece of paper on the floor to represent the wall space you want to fill with pictures. Arrange the pictures on the paper, outline the frames, mark the paper for hook placement. Tape the paper to the wall and hang hooks. Remove the paper and hang pictures.

COLOR SCHEMES AND SAMPLES

Order samples of fabric, wallpaper, and carpet, each a yard in length. Never choose items from tiny swatches. Tape wallpaper to walls and live with it a few days before deciding. When selecting paint, bring home paint chips to check the color in your home light. If you are painting a large wall area, an intense color will appear more intense. A pastel shade will look darker on a wall than on a paint chip.

If your room looks rather dull and you want to liven it up a bit, paint or antique a trunk, cabinet, or any piece of furniture a bright color. If you like contemporary furniture, choose shiny, smooth drapery fabrics. If the country look is your favorite, select dull soft textures (not dull colors!)—cottons, and so on. If you choose inexpensive fabric, choose a solid color.

A solid-color floor covering allows you to choose patterned paper and fabrics that match or harmonize. Use the background color of print draperies for the walls and repeat the print's other hues in upholstery, pillows, and other accessories.

Make a swatch card to take on shopping trips. Staple onto a three-by-five-inch card small samples of fabrics, threads of carpet, and wallpaper. Take some Popsicle sticks and paint them the color of your walls or of furniture you have painted. (See priority notebook section for more ideas.)

KEEP A ROOM SIMPLE

Keep a room simple and rotate your collections and accessories. Do not try to fill every corner with furniture and appurtenances. Underdecorate a room rather than overdecorate it.

PLAN, PREPARE A ROOM, AND TAKE ACTION!

Paint the closets and the inside of cabinets first. While the room is being painted and wallpapered, you can take a few breaks and use the time to arrange the shelves and closet space.

Put some leftover paint from your rooms in small air-tight jars. Label the jars. Keep these in a handy storage space. When you get a mark on the wall or if the paint chips, dip a cotton swab in the paint to touch up the damaged areas.

Remember, decorating takes time, patience, and good planning. Do not expect to get everything the way you want it overnight. It will come in time, and you will appreciate it more if you have had to wait.

VISUAL IMAGES REINFORCE YOUR VALUES AND GOALS

Our surroundings can remind us of what is truly important in our lives. Visual images in our homes probably influence us more than we realize.

Every home should have several bulletin boards. Each child's room should have a large one, and there should be at least one large one in the family area, too. We lined one side of a kitchen cupboard from floor to ceiling with cork and covered one kitchen wall with a six-by-four-foot sheet of cellutex framed with pine cornice board. This bulletin board cost less than ten dollars, and it has been an invaluable aid in family living and learning.

Our family has adopted three missionary families with whom

we stay in contact and support financially. On our large bulletin board we have a world map. Small flags pinned to Taiwan, El Salvador, and Kenya show us at a glance where our missionaries live and work. We also have photographs of the missionary families pinned to the map, near where they live. This is an everyday reminder of our friends who labor for Christ overseas.

Visual images reflect our faith in Christ:

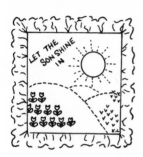 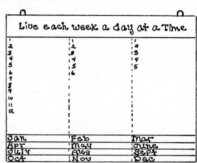

Kathie's daughter Stacy made this pillow for her room. Everything in that room, which was wallpapered with yellow and white checks, radiated the joy of Jesus Christ. Stacy also designed a three-months-at-a-glance calendar for her wall. Her calendar gave her the visual reminder she needed to be organized and responsible.

This wall plaque leaves no question about the Lidens' commitment as a family.

A talented Christian young woman made this hanging for friends when their baby arrived. The banner hangs on the door of the child's room and will be treasured for a lifetime.

Visual images strengthen family ties:

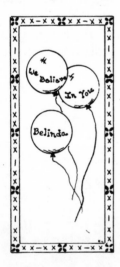

Kathie made these plaques for her daughters, Stacy and Belinda.

You may use hall space to put up yearly pictures of each child. Annual school pictures cost very little. It is great fun to watch the children grow from babyhood to their present age. They love it, and so do their friends.

Use bulletin boards to hang family collages, awards, posters honoring family members, and any other material that comes from family night activities. We made a family mobile from shrink art. It hangs from our kitchen ceiling. It contains many symbols of what our family means to us: a picture of Linus and his blanket titled "Security," a heart with the word "love" on it, a Bible, a parakeet, a dog and a cat (our pets), and so on.

Harry and Gwen Hurlburt, very active outdoor people, bought a large map of California and hung it on their kitchen bulletin board. When they took family trips, they traced their routes on the map with dark colors. Alongside the map they pinned photographs showing members of the family at various times and places on the trips. The family and their friends enjoyed this visual reminder of the Hurlburts' travels.

The Hurlburts also put up pictures of birds the family was learning about, Indian artifacts they had picked up in their travels, nutritional news, and so on. Gwen and Harry turned their home into an exciting place where everyone could learn something every day.

Stores sell a frame that has matted slots for eight or ten photographs. You could use this kind of frame to keep a current visual reminder of pleasant family activities. You might also use it to display pictures of houses in which the family has lived.

Many other items remind the family of its uniqueness and its heritage—family heirlooms, old pictures, posters, plaques, paintings, and much more. Use every opportunity you can to strengthen family values by using visual reminders. These displays of family interests and activities go a long way toward transforming your house into a warm, stimulating home.

MAKE AN INSPECTION TOUR

Creating physical order within the house involves a room-by-room inspection to see if anything can be done to make the house more functional. Once a room is under control in terms of organization, it is relatively simple to keep it in running order.

It is impossible to follow the old adage "A place for everything and everything in its place" unless we have maximized the functional potential of every room. Special thought must be given to creating the "places" necessary to keep everything and make order easy.

If your house does not have adequate cupboard and closet space, invest in some inexpensive unfinished chests, cabinets, or shelving. Some houses do have physical limitations, but see what you can do to relieve the crowded conditions by sorting, filing, and throwing away excess belongings.

Built-in storage may be one answer. You can fit closets and drawers into many corners where conventional furniture would not go. You can plan them to use space near the floor (under seats, beds, or work surfaces) or near the ceiling. You can find lots of space going to waste if you look for it.

Before you make any decisions, take a tour of the house, and as you go, ask yourselves these questions: What do we do in this room? What do we need here? Is there anything here that belongs in another room? Is there anything in another room that belongs here? How can we improve this room so that it can do better what it is supposed to do?

COMING IN FROM OUTDOORS

The Lidens raised the pole in their entryway closet so two "clutter shelves" could be placed near the floor. They covered the shelves with cherry checked Contact paper. Belinda and Stacy kept their things on the bottom shelf, and Dave and Kathie used the upper shelf. This clutter center received top priority once a week for cleaning and sorting.

Some of the things they put on these shelves: library books that needed to be returned; items borrowed from friends, that had been placed in paper bags labeled with the lenders' names; school

books, supplies, and lunches or lunch money; extra maps or survey equipment brought home from the office; bags of purchases until they could be sorted and put away later; gifts or other miscellaneous items they must not forget to take with them when on their way out the front door.

On the closet door was a mug rack, hung low for purses and small children's sweaters and coats. A small shoe bag stored mittens, knitted hats, the dog leash, and a clothes brush.

The blank wall space on the inside of the closet was used to hang extra supplies. Several toy bags made of bright checked gingham stored soft toys, puzzles, and coloring books and crayons. A bag of building blocks was most popular with visiting small children. Umbrellas hung on hooks. The other side of the closet had hooks to hold tennis rackets.

Most families with active children have sports equipment going in and out of the house frequently. A trunk near the door will fit in with planning storage according to family activities. The garage may be a more logical storage place, but getting family members to detour through the garage can result in unnecessary nagging.

The trunk can also be used to sit on when taking off wet shoes. Hang a mirror close by to check your smile before walking out the door.

Near a back door put an old dish drainer. Place it on several thicknesses of old newspaper and place wet boots in it to drain. When the boots are dry, roll up the newspaper and discard. Another good parking place for wet boots and umbrellas is a big box lined with a plastic place mat. To clean, just go over the mat with a damp cloth.

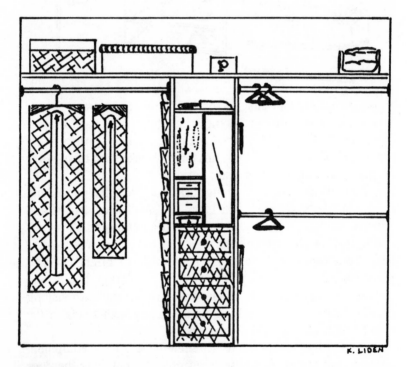

K. LIDEN

BEDROOMS

Make the bedroom closet more space saving by adding partitions, shelves, boxes, and double-tiered hanging rods for shirts, blouses, jackets, and skirts. Make the shelves of various widths so things can be stored one deep—narrowest at the top, widest at the bottom. Wallpaper the inside of the closet if it needs brightening.

Use a small pine or fabric-covered cardboard chest of drawers (portable) to store nylons, underwear, et cetera. On top of the chest set a small, clear plastic set of three drawers (available at the hardware store) and line it with a thin sheet of foam rubber so large pieces of jewelry do not slide around. Above these drawers you may fasten a piece of painted pegboard for hanging watches and long-chained accessories.

In the other half of the space above your chest of drawers, arrange shelves. A mirror from the dime store can slide back and forth for getting behind the other side of the shelves. She can have one side, and he can have the other.

You can make a compartment for purses (extra one for trading off during the season). Use a clear plastic box on the top shelf as a sorting box for different purses and accessories. Use clear boxes for gloves, scarves, handkerchiefs, ribbons, and the like.

A free-standing metal shoe rack (which men prefer to the open kind) can slide under the garment bags. On the inside wall of the closet hang two shoe bags (twenty-four pockets) to hold her shoes and clothes brushes, shoe brushes, extra knitted caps, and gloves. A flashlight for emergency fits here nicely along with several cakes of unwrapped soap to add fragrance to the closet. Tuck in a small note pad and pencil too, so you can write down ideas and needs as you think of them.

Attach a towel bar inside the closet or on the door for belts, ties, or scarves. If you have closet doors that open into the room, attach a full-length mirror.

Store sweaters in plastic vegetable bins. Store off-season clothing in storage boxes under the bed. Drawers built under a bed are convenient for storing heavy clothing, blankets, sports equipment, and so on. Some people use empty suitcases for this purpose. Ski and fishing clothes can go in storage boxes in the garage or attic.

K. LIDEN

Brighten children's closets by wallpapering the inside with cute prints and gaily painted shelves. If you have closet doors that open into the room, attach shoe bags, see-me-grow charts, cute sayings, and blackboards for reminders of needs. Blackboard Contact paper is now available in many stores. Hang one blackboard high—for parents to use—and one low for the children to draw on.

Place a few clothes (tops and bottoms together) on a low pole so children can choose the outfit of the day. Rotate clothes from the higher pole so children are not confused with too much to choose from. Store socks and underwear in a low dishpan for easy reach. Pajamas can easily be hung on low hooks. Add a few extra hooks for play sweaters and light jackets. Young children can care for a dressing center such as this because everything is within their reach and control.

Put a hamper in every bedroom. The "hamper" can be a cardboard carton covered with Contact paper. Teach the child to turn his dirty clothes to the right side (no inside-out, wadded-up socks) before placing them in the hamper.

Code sheets by color and store them in bedroom closets. If you have two children sharing a room, each should have his own color. Color code hair brushes, hangers (wrap colored adhesive tape around the neck of the hanger), and other personal belongings.

Hang large bulletin boards in children's bedrooms. They will also need bookshelves to store their books.

For handy inexpensive toy bins, invest in several colored dishpans and one soft dustpan to match. Color code for each child. When pick-up time arrives, the child will enjoy scooping up small toys with his soft dustpan. Dishpans are portable. Take them along on short or long trips. They also store children's drawings and school papers well.

Hang larger toys by sewing plastic rings on the tops. Place hooks in an easy-to-reach spot so children can put away their own toys.

Take a toy inventory and find out what your children play with most often. When the children are absent, go through the toy box. Separate the toys into dishpans according to go-togethers—building blocks for forts with horses and cowboys, and so on. Put to rest the toys they do not play with and any toys they have not been taking care of. Store two or three dishpans on lower shelves where children can easily reach them. The others go on the top shelf from where they can be rotated as the children tire of toys. Toys that are put to rest can be stored in the garage or attic until you want to reactivate them.

BATHROOM

Add extra cabinets or shelves high on the wall and above the toilet. Use organizers, shower caddy, utensil dividers, and so on to keep supplies in order. Build shelves in the cavity of the sink cabinet, either fitted around the pipes or along the sides, to hold extra tissues, soap, toothpaste, and cleaning supplies. Add a shelf on which members of the family can keep their own makeup baskets.

Hang a shoe bag on the back of the bathroom door to store shavers, hair rollers, and other supplies. Also have hooks on the door.

Hang a pad and pencil on the bathroom wall. Use the pad to request more supplies when they run low. Hang a wine rack to hold rolled towels. Fasten glass and toothbrush holders to the wall or inside the vanity cabinet door. Glasses may be color coded.

Prevent the problem of towels on the floor by putting some snaps or Velcro on them. Hang the towels low enough for the children to use.

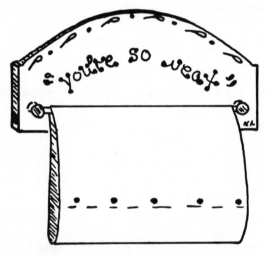

Assign each child a towel bar that is large enough to hold his bath towel and wet wash cloth. Towels and wash cloths can be color coded. When you find a wet towel on the floor (it happens!), you will know to whom it belongs.

A clock in the bathroom can help keep the family on time. Every bathroom should also have a wastebasket. Provide a step stool so small children can reach the sink.

Make a net bag to hold bath toys. Hang it over the tub where the toys can drip dry. A net ball is great for children to use to clean the tub. It dries quickly. Keep a sponge handy for spills and to wipe the metal strip at the bottom of the shower door. Hang a drying rack above the shower or tub for bathing suits, hand washing, and so on.

For safety provide a night light. Locks should be the type that can be opened from the outside in emergency. Keep electrical appliances away from water. Put a small dot of nail polish on the hot water faucet.

A hand shower attachment is helpful for rinsing off muddy children and for washing hair in the tub. If you do not have children, use it to wash off your ivy.

To keep their shampoo, rinses, and razors handy, invest in a small bucket for each teen. It can be taken into the shower or used as a tote. It can also be used to wash out underwear quickly. Keep a small bottle of dishwashing soap in the bathroom for just such occasions.

KITCHEN

On an inspection tour we cannot do much more than check to see how streamlined our own rooms are. Now that you have reached the kitchen, look for the basic work centers. Have you organized your cupboards and drawers to make work easier in each center? Have you cut steps to an absolute minimum?

Open the cupboard doors and the drawers. Do you keep only the tools you use constantly, or are there freeloaders? Do your most-used dishes, pans, and utensils occupy prime space? Front and center shelf and drawer space must be reserved for prime property. Unless you use an item every day, it does not deserve front space.

Plan your kitchen to save steps. Think in terms of these basic work centers: the range or cooking center, the sink and clean-up center, and the food preparation and serving center. Plan drawer space at each work center.

Mixing and Food Preparation

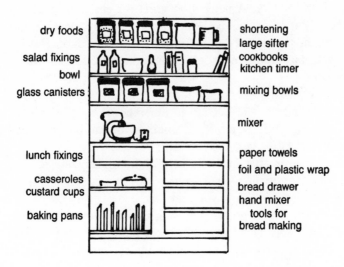

dry foods — shortening / large sifter

salad fixings — cookbooks / kitchen timer

bowl

glass canisters — mixing bowls

— mixer

lunch fixings — paper towels / foil and plastic wrap

casseroles / custard cups — bread drawer / hand mixer

baking pans — tools for bread making

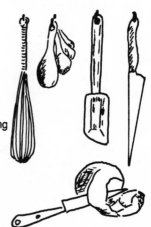

- At least 36 inches of counter space
- Use inside cabinet door space (attach hanging spice racks, bins for salt, pepper)
- 1-cup and 4-cup glass measuring cups for liquid measuring
- Cutting board on counter

Keep small tools within easy reach, like hanging under shelves or on a tool board
- 2 sets of metal measuring cups and spoons
- grater
- potato peeler
- hand can opener
- kitchen scissors
- bottle opener
- medium wire whisk
- two rubber spatulas
- *Most important* . . . a sharp *paring knife,* and slicing and chopping knife

The cooking center. The cooking center should have an oven, heat-resistant counters next to the burners, and pot holders that are fire resistant. Keep duplicate seasonings most used (salt, pepper, flour) here too. Some people like to keep their toasters and slow cookers on the counter next to the range. If you use a microwave oven, you will want to store paper towels and plates in the cooking area.

Basic cookware includes: a two quart saucepan, a six to eight quart saucepan for cooking spaghetti and noodles, an iron skillet, a Teflon skillet for eggs, a five quart dutch oven with lid, and, if you are soup lovers, a big pot.

Install pegboard and hooks to hang tools and a portable cutting board. Tools include wooden spoons, tongs, metal wire whisk, spatula, ladle, pancake turner, cooking fork, slotted spoon, basting spoon, strainer, spoon rest, cooking thermometers, and duplicate measuring cups and spoons if preparation center is some distance from cooking center.

The sink area. Store dishwashing soap and cleaner close to the sink. A drawer can hold soap pads, cleaning sponges, a nylon or stainless steel scrubber, vegetable and bottle brushes. Leave your dish drainer in the sink for handy use when washing vegetables.

Keep coffeepot and coffee near the sink. Keep measuring scoop inside coffee canister. Make a mug holder with hooks. Each family member has a mug for getting drinks during the day.

Paint the inside of the space under the sink a bright color to reflect light. Slide-out drawers and vegetable bins make use of this space. Hang a colander and extra strainers on hooks. Attach a towel rack to the inside of the cabinet door for drying towels and hanging wet gloves. You may want to keep your kitchen waste-basket under the sink.

Serving center. Separate glasses and dishes you use daily. In the serving center keep one setting for each person, bowls for vegetables, and a platter. Store table linens and silverware in a drawer in the serving center. Save money by making a dozen cloth napkins to use regularly. Hang place mats on a clip inside a cabinet door.

Shallow shelves may be better for storage than deep ones. Install shallow halfway cabinets or shelves between counter top and wall cabinets to store small items. Use turntables or lazy Susans on deep shelves or in corner cabinets.

A magnetic knife rack to store knives, and magnetic hooks for other kitchen utensils, save space. Use wall space for other wall-mounted dispensers and portable appliances as well. Attach small containers or racks to the inside of kitchen cabinet doors for envelope mixes and other small hard-to-store items.

Spice racks will make space available in wall cabinets. Keep often-used spices in the preparation center. Store seldom-used spices in less accessible space. Ideally, spices should be stored away from heat, moisture, and light. If tightly covered, herbs will keep about a year and a half and ground spices for about two years. Give each spice the "aroma" test. If there is no smell, there is no taste left.

Add a kitchen island to gain more work and storage space. If you can convert a space into a pantry, you are very fortunate. Every kitchen should have an old-fashioned pantry. Be sure to find a wall or the side of a cabinet to put up a bulletin board, or cover with cork tile.

A terry cloth apron with pockets is a good cover-up for splatters while cooking. You can also use it to wipe or dry your hands.

LIVING AND DINING ROOMS
End tables with storage space, hollow hassocks, buffets,

sideboards, and other furniture that makes available storage area will help provide the places you need to store your belongings. A restored old trunk will add interest as well as storage space.

Adjustable shelves are inexpensive and are useful for storing books, electronic equipment, and collectors' items. If you have no other place for them, store table linens in large shallow boxes under the sofa.

Provide a basket or magazine rack for current newspapers and magazines. These can also be stored in the cabinet of end tables.

GARAGE AND ALTERNATE STORAGE AREAS

Closets take care of many items around the house, but as the years go by you find you have leftover things that do not seem to fit anywhere. You do not want to throw them away, but you cannot seem to find them when you need them.

Living quarters are smaller, and attics, spare rooms, basements, barns, and sheds are hard to come by. Most houses have garages, many have limited attic space, and portable garden sheds are available everywhere. You will have to make the most of what you have available to you.

Sue has converted a small attic into a useful storage area. The attic is not high enough for standing up straight, but the high pitch of the roof gives almost enough room. Sue and her husband, Josh, laid plywood floors and hooked up a fluorescent light from the hallway wall switch.

From a department store catalog Sue ordered a kit containing a disappearing stairway. She and Josh installed the stairway through an opening in the hall ceiling. They pull a string, and the stairway comes down from the attic into the hall.

Josh and Sue's small storage room holds many items. A sports area contains skis, baseball mitts, badminton and tennis gear, and a bicycle pump. One storage box holds games. There is a record player they take to church parties. There are boxes of costumes. Other boxes contain holiday supplies. One area contains baby clothes and resting toys. There is a gift section holding boxes, white elephants for parties, wrapping paper, and ribbon. There are even small antiques waiting to be refinished.

A two-shelf bookcase holds books, special event newspapers, travel maps, and extra business forms. Sue and Josh use as many clear plastic containers as they can to store their things. They have the pull-out-drawer type and the shoe-box variety.

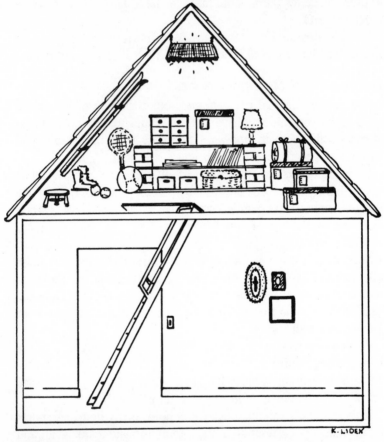

Garages offer endless possibilities for storage. The secret to good garage storage is to have a workable system of labeling so that you know where everything is at all times. There are a number of ways to do this.

You can make a master list and number the boxes. If you use

this method, be sure to make several copies of the master list and post them in two or three different places.

Another method is to tape a four-by-five- or five-by-seven-inch card to each box and list the contents. Larger cards are easier to see, of course. You may also use see-through containers. No labeling is needed for these.

Open metal shelf units provide organized storage for cartons of Christmas decorations, picnic gear, beauty items, costumes, and so on. Metal cabinets are a good place for extra canned goods, paint, and painting equipment.

Organize nails, nuts, bolts, and so on in small metal and plastic cabinets having lots of mini-drawers. A discarded lunch pail will store small tools nicely and is conveniently portable. Screw-top jars can be nailed by the top to the underside of shelves to hold nails, screws, et cetera.

Pegboard, shelves, and cabinets are all essential for efficient garage storage. Hang tools, garden chairs, and much more from hooks on the pegboard. Use overhead space to store large items. Put boards across the rafters to make a flat surface.

Apple and orange boxes make excellent storage cartons. Toilet tissue boxes are good for large items. You can also buy large brightly colored storage boxes for about one dollar.

Sometimes you may save time by putting often-used things together rather than storing like things together. The following are examples of what your master list might include.

Master List

Box 1—Beauty and Health
permanent rollers
heat cap
ice bag
heating pad
extra hair clips
hairstyling book
hair scissors and razor
plastic cape for hair cuts
(Related items)

Box 2
glue (white)
masking tape
string
black ink (drawing)
cheesecloth
clear Contact paper
tacks
(Unrelated items)

Or, label contents on the boxes using four-by-six-or five-by-seven-inch cards:

Hobby Supplies
cheesecloth
brushes
small canvas
steel wool
fine sandpaper
tracing paper

Miscellaneous Items
joke gifts for friends and parties
gift boxes
small frames
picture wire

Wrapping Paper and Supplies
gift paper
ribbon
string
brown mailing paper
mailing envelopes
labels

LAUNDRY AND CLEANING CENTER

To turn your laundry space into a convenient work center, build a plywood unit to slide over the dryer. One side has two shelves to give you extra soap storage or hang a pull-out guide for hanging brushes and extra tools. The right side has colored dishpans for clean clothes. When they are full, each person puts away his own clothes and returns the pan. Color code the dishpans.

The top of the slide-over unit gives you plenty of room for folding clothes or for placing a pressing pad on top for quick touch-ups. Provide a storage place for a portable ironing pad.

Hangers may be placed on a long hook, or attach a towel bar under the shelf for quick storage and pickup. A big glass jar houses your measuring cup and soap. Paper towels are handy for quick wipe-ups. Several cups are hung on hooks for measuring bleach and softener. Store bleach out of reach of children.

Keep a file box for washing instructions. Tape garment tabs (washing instructions) on three-by-five-inch cards and put in the file box.

Provide a clear jar for buttons and other lost-and-found items, and a dishpan for clean rags. A small bucket is useful for hand

washings and a larger one can be used as a tote for daily cleaning supplies. A "fix it" list goes on a small clipboard and can be carried in the tote bucket.

Place hooks on the side of the partition for clothes to be hung up immediately after removing from the dryer. Attach a towel bar for hanging pants and other flat items. A drying rack is great for things that cannot go in the dryer.

An eighteen-by-twenty-four-inch pegboard holds a small tool kit. Paper, scissors, masking tape, string, and an extra set of house keys go on this board. A small tray holds white glue, pencils, colored adhesive tape, and iron-on tape for clothes identification.

Hang dirty rags on a small piece of clothesline until washday. Several extra sets of gloves hang there, too. Hang your broom and dustpan. Keep extra sets upstairs and in the garage. Keep a wastebasket close for disposal of empty containers and lint.

That completes the inspection tour. As you go through your own house, jot down ideas for streamlining each room to make it do what it is supposed to do.

4

Manage the Minute

Jesus told a story about a man who left home to take a trip. For the time he was gone he entrusted his possessions to his servants. To one he gave five talents, to another two, and to another one, each according to his own ability.

The first one traded with his talents and gained five more. The second, through industry, also doubled his talents. The third dug a hole and buried his talent so that he could return it intact to his master.

When the master returned, he praised the two servants who had invested his money wisely, but he became very angry with the servant who did not use the talent he had been given.

Do you realize that we, too, have been given talents? Each of us is unique—a one-time happening. No one in history is exactly like you. You have skills, interests, temperament, and experience that make you uniquely individual.

Learning to manage time effectively involves finding out how you are special and that it is relatively easy to do. Think about yourself. Some things come easily to you, and you like to do

61

them. You have characteristics that friends have mentioned or that you have recognized in yourself. These traits come naturally to you. Perhaps you find math easy. Or you like to be with people. Or you are easygoing and can handle situations in which other people become restless and impatient. You may be slow moving, meticulous. You may have a sister or brother who is retarded, and you have learned to be supportive of her or him.

These skills, interests, emotions, and experiences make you what you are. They could be called your natural bent, your God-given gifts, your strengths. Concentrate on these strengths. God never intended you to bury them. Dig them up. Take a look at them. Now see what you can do to bring them to life.

God created each of us for a special purpose, and our responsibility is to find that purpose—to become what we already are. Does that make sense? It means developing our potential, or investing the talents God has given us.

I am not convinced that God rigidly sets one specific, detailed plan for your life, and alas! if you make a wrong choice and forever miss the chance to do what He had in mind. Rather, He gives choices. If you do not marry that young person headed for foreign missions, for which you might have been well-suited, God has another person in mind or another opportunity for you to develop your God-given potential. So cheer up! Look for God's plan for you right now.

Everyone has 24 hours a day and 168 hours a week to become what he or she should become. Some people have 85 years or more. Others, like Jesus, have much less than that. The only time that really matters is right now. Are you making the best use of your time right now?

WHAT TIME-MANAGEMENT EXPERTS TEACH

Time management experts such as Ari Kiev, Edwin G. Bliss, Donna Goldfein, Alan Lakein, and Peter Drucker have slightly different approaches to using time effectively, but their advice all boils down to the same basic principles. We want to take a look at those principles and apply them to this challenge of becoming what God has made it possible for us to be.

FIRST, SET PRIORITIES.

Many people believe that if they could extend each day by a couple of hours, that would solve all their problems. Actually, none of us has a shortage of time. Our problem is failing to sort out priorities.

You may be the most efficient person on your block, but if you spend your time doing things of little consequence, all your efficiency counts for nothing. It reminds me of the football player who intercepted a pass and carried the football with great speed and expertise ninety yards to the wrong goal.

Many husbands and fathers are like this football player. They throw themselves into their work, using all their energy and most of their time earning a living. They may be tremendously efficient, but how effective is a husband and father who loses his own family?

In marriage one of the greatest sources of conflict is determining how priorities should be set. Dr. David Olson and Dr. Dana Olson, marital and family therapists in Minneapolis, teach couples to divide time into "I-time" and "we-time." Many couples would have to include another category for time with the children.

It is important to recognize our interdependence as well as our need to be individuals. You can help by allowing each to pursue his own direction as well as to share activities. When setting priorities, allow couple-time, I-time, and children-time. Each is important.

Determine your priorities. What do you want to do with your life? What is important to you?

SECOND, LIST YOUR GOALS.

You may want to take ten minutes each day for ten days to list ten possible goals. Ask yourself, Where am I going? How do I want to live? What do I want to accomplish in my career, education, family, religion, finances, and physical well-being? At the end of the ten days go over the list and pick out the three most important goals and number them in order of importance to you.

THIRD, LIST STEPS TO TAKE TOWARD GOAL ACHIEVEMENT.

Ask yourself what you must do to reach each goal. List small, easy steps you can take minute by minute or day by day that will propel you in the right direction. The key is to make these tasks short and easy, so that you can get started right away and accomplish them.

You will have to consider questions such as when to start, what to do first, what information and equipment you will need, who else will be involved, and how much time you can spend working toward goal achievement each day. Think through the steps you will take along the way to achieving your goal. Practice, using your imagination.

On a three-by-five-inch card, list your major objective, and the three immediate steps you plan to take to reach it. Carry the card in your pocket. Look at it throughout the day. Place a copy in your priority notebook in the "Daily Checklist" or "Personal Prayer" section.

To visualize the objective even more clearly, add to your card a picture that symbolizes your goal. You can cut the picture out of a magazine or book. If you keep the goal clearly in mind each day, it will not seem like a dream. It will become an achievable reality.

Remember to "follow your dreams, for as you dream so shall you become" (James Allen).

FOURTH, PLAN.

Few people would think of taking a trip without first making preparations for it. Those preparations would include getting and studying road maps, checking costs and availability of funds, making sure there is reliable transportation and whatever is needed to have a good time, perhaps making reservations, and estimating how much time will be allotted for each phase of the trip.

Is it not strange that many people who carefully plan a vacation trip are traveling the greatest journey of all—life—with virtually no preparation or plans. If you do not know where you are going, it really does not matter which road you take, but you should realize that you risk dead ends, frustration, and even disaster.

To make good plans, you need to know where you are going. Setting priorities, goals, and steps necessary to reach those goals will clearly define where you are going. To carry out these activities you must continually plan.

Are you a list maker? You should be. Take ten minutes every evening to make a "To Do" list for the next day. Be sure your list breaks jobs into small segments. For example, you should not write "clean house." Instead, break the housecleaning into less overwhelming, bite-size tasks such as "dust the living area."

Go over the list and assign priorities to each item. I like to number mine. Some people who have tried this say they get hung up on trying to decide whether one thing is more important than another. If this is your problem, assign priority by category using the A-B-C or the 1-2-3 method. Assign A or 1 to high priority items, B or 2 to next highest, and C or 3 to those of low priority. Always star the most important activity on your list so that you will have a place to begin each day.

If you do not get around to B and C items, do not worry. Today's C item may become an A item tomorrow, and you will not have wasted your time today on what could very well be done tomorrow. Your "To Do" list will keep you doing first things first, and that will guarantee an effective use of time.

FIFTH, LIVE IN THE HERE AND NOW.

Your activity will move you toward your goal, and it is that activity that matters. Neither the future nor the past are of any importance except as they relate to now. Do not waste time or energy worrying about what may happen or what has happened. Failures teach us what action to avoid. Anyone who does anything learns through failure. If you never fail, you are not doing anything.

Build on your successes and put your failures behind you. To dwell on failures drains you of faith and energy. God gives each living person a new day every twenty-four hours. Rejoice in that new beginning and take advantage of it. Today is all that really matters.

SIXTH, CONCENTRATE ON ONE THING AT A TIME.

When I first began writing books, I thought I would continue writing magazine articles as well. I soon learned that the only way I could succeed at either activity was to do one at a time.

Concentrate on the activity you have given top priority on your list. Mentally blot out all the others. When you finish the most important one, you can go on to number two. If you cannot do everything on your list, relax. You know you are doing the most important things first, and tomorrow is another day and another list.

SEVENTH, BE FLEXIBLE.

Review your goals from time to time. Feel free to abandon a goal or to set a new one. It is hoped we all change and grow. What may have been important at thirty, may not be important at forty. A person who never grows or changes is stagnant and cannot develop his potential. Persevere when you know your goal is right, but do not be afraid to update and change your plans.

EIGHTH, CONSULT YOUR DIVINE PARTNER OFTEN.

I am adding this eighth principle, because I think it is essential to managing a Christian home. Through prayer and studying God's Word, you will have an advantage in setting priorities. A person in tune with God usually has his priorities straight. Faith will help you to stick to a goal based on those priorities for as long as it takes to achieve it.

Prayer can help control self-defeating and impulsive reactions to anxiety. Prayer will increase your faith in your own ability to achieve your God-given objectives. It will give you strength to endure frustrations and uncertainty.

Objectivity comes through prayer. Thank God for your strengths. Think about Him and His many attributes. Now realize that in Jesus Christ you are His child. You are made in His image. He has promised you His strength. With such an awesome source of power, how can you waste time thinking about your inadequacy? Let Him help you to become what He has already made you.

If you follow these eight steps, you will give your life direction. You will become what you are capable of becoming. You will face the excitement of challenge, growth, and a meaningful life.

LEARN TO SAY NO

At eleven o'clock in the morning Marilyn looked around the kitchen in despair. She had just finished feeding two-months-old Shauna, cereal had dried on breakfast dishes that filled the sink, and several beds were unmade. She had not written to her parents since sending the announcement of Shauna's birth. She had promised Judy she would finish her costume for the party tonight, and her husband, Don, had asked her to pay some bills and run some errands for him. She had also planned going to a Bible study at her neighbor's house right after lunch.

"I've got too much to do, and I don't know where to begin," she said aloud. She fought back tears.

That night Don came home to a messy house, cranky children, and an unhappy wife. "I just can't get everything done," she told him.

In another part of the country, Joe also had a bad day. A score of interruptions kept him from getting one thing done on a project his employer had labeled urgent. He had participated in three meetings, skipped lunch, and come to the end of the day feeling like he had been on a treadmill, constantly moving but never going anywhere. He came home late and swallowed supper in record time, barely grunting to his family before hurrying to the church for a committee meeting on "meeting the family's needs in the church."

While sitting in the meeting he wondered, *Why do I take on so much responsibility? Why don't I ever have time to do the things I think are really important?*

Both Marilyn and Joe are among the thousands of people having "too much to do." We live in a world that makes innumerable demands on an individual's time and resources. You must take responsibility for determining what you are going to do. Assess every activity in terms of your priorities. Will this activity move you toward your goals or will it divert your energy and attention from those goals?

The key here is to be in tune with God's will for your life. Too often people divert their energies and become ineffective in the work God has for them simply because they try to be all things to all men. In order to live an effective Christian life, a person must be "in charge" under God's direction.

There are many reasons people do not feel comfortable saying no. It may simply be habit to allow others to take the responsibility for running your life. You may automatically take on a job that you realize must be done. You may lack confidence and constantly try to buy friendship by doing things for others. Perhaps you relish the feeling of indispensability that comes with having a reputation for always getting the job done. You know your fellow workers wonder how they would ever get along without you. Whatever the reason, the consequence is the same: you do not run your life under God's direction; you allow others to run it for you.

If you value time, you cannot afford to squander it by always doing what others want you to do. You must learn to say no to requests for favors you can ill afford to give and to activities that divert your energy in many directions. You must be selective in accepting invitations or commitments.

Take a look at the daily pressures in your life. What activities are draining you? To what extent are you neglecting your own needs and goals? Focus, too, on your attitudes toward other people. Are you too concerned about what they think of you? Are you afraid of criticism? Do you have a compulsion for perfection?

To gain control, look for the times you behave according to how others expect you to behave, or when you agree to an activity because you wish to avoid the discomfort of saying no. Try responding differently the next time you find yourself in this situation.

Trust your friends, co-workers, and family to support you, whatever your reasons for not helping. Be willing to risk criticism and even anger as you allow others to assume responsibility that rightfully belongs to them. This gives them the freedom to live their lives as God intended, too.

Take time to make decisions. If you are asked to serve in some new capacity, ask for time to think and pray about it. This will give you the opportunity to evaluate the request in terms of your broader objectives. Delay will help you to assess priorities and to decrease your vulnerability. After seeking God's guidance, you can feel good about your decision and free from fear or anxiety about it.

If you do not want to do something, say so outright. Do not make excuses. Do not answer with hesitation. If you say, "Well," or, "I don't know," you will be subjected to great pressure to say yes.

At first, you may feel uncomfortable with your new freedom, but more and more you will discover the exhilaration of taking charge of your life and living it the way you know God intends you to live. Keep trying. Plan time for the activities necessary to reach your goal. You can give away your free time as you choose.

Involvement in any activity should suit your interests and time schedule and come from genuine desire and a sense of God's will. With you and God in charge of your life, you know where you are going and how best to get there. It is the only way you can become what God intended you to become—the one-of-a-kind person He made you.

MAKE THE MINUTE WORK FOR YOU

To many people a minute is like a penny. One is not worth picking up. But if you put enough of them together they become valuable.

Unfortunately, many of us lose a great many minutes, because we have not yet learned that a little time goes a long way. If you think of bits and pieces of time as opportunities for action, you can use them productively.

I used to fritter away five-minute segments of time, because five minutes was too little time to start something, and I believed nothing of any importance could be done in five minutes. Recently I took on the challenge of discovering what can be done in just five minutes.

Here is what I have discovered I can do in five minutes: clean a bathroom sink, do a great many exercises, write a thank-you note, plan a meal, set the table, make an appointment, feed the pets, water the plants, make the bed, or read a chapter in the Bible.

At any time of the day, use spare minutes to take care of necessary tasks. Take a look at your "To Do" list. If you have broken the tasks into small parts, you can always find bits and pieces of activity to fit your available segment of time. Time yourself at your tasks. You may find that cleaning the medicine cabinet takes only ten minutes, a segment of time you often have.

Sometimes you can make minutes count by doubling up. Here are examples:

Cut two outfits of different fabrics from the same pattern and use the same color of thread in the machine. You can sew up two skirts in about the same time it takes to make one.

Listen to tapes or memorize verses while driving. Make out a shopping list, or review your priority notebook while riding the bus.

Write letters while waiting for doctors or dentists. Always keep a supply of postcards in your purse. Straighten the kitchen while giving the kids a snack. Do exercises or wash clothes while dinner cooks.

Set the table with dishes from the dishwasher. Eliminate the task of putting them in the cupboard. Never go from one part of the house to another with empty hands. Add a little bleach when soaking linens or plastic bowls in your sink. It cleans the sink at the same time.

Double your dinner recipe. Freeze half of it for another meal.

Do all your entertaining in one week. The house is clean, and you can use the same flowers, shop at one time, and so on.

Have a project or manicure tools near the telephone. Work on the project or file your nails while talking. If you have a long cord on your telephone, you can cook, bake, or clean the sink while talking.

Respect the minute. See how many of them you can find. You will find them in strange places. I find some extra minutes in the evenings while my family watches television shows I do not particularly enjoy. I use that time to do the things that do not rate prime time in my daily schedule. Sometimes I simply pamper myself. I sit down with a book I have been wanting to read, or I soak in a nice warm bath.

The wise use of television can save many valuable minutes. We all need time to relax, but how you relax should be determined by choice, not by habit or by what is on at the moment. Our children came up with a solution to television watching that solved two problems at once. They suggested we each pay five cents for every half hour of television we watch. We use the money for family projects we all select by vote. We were surprised at how few television shows are worth a nickel. These days our television set is off more often than it is on.

One woman found the time she needed in the morning. "I loved to sleep in the morning, but I knew I should be getting up earlier," she says. "So I took a few small steps at a time. First, I got up and stayed up. The ten minute nap I allowed myself at nine o'clock lasted for three weeks. Then I substituted exercise at 9:00, and I found I had added a new dimension to my life."

You may be getting more sleep than you need. If so, you may find you can add an hour to your day without making yourself feel more tired. An hour a day is 7 hours a week, 365 hours a year, and 3650 hours in ten years. That is a lot of time!

Minutes are time, and time is life. If you can find more of it to do the things you want to do, you have given yourself a priceless gift.

Work "Smarter"

Let us consider four ways to work "smarter" and thereby manage the minute more effectively.

DEVELOP AND MAINTAIN A PROFESSIONAL ATTITUDE TOWARD YOUR WORK.

Your attitude toward your work, whether it is housecleaning or writing a book, makes the difference in how you manage your time. If you do not value the job, you will do it any old way, any old time, and that certainly will not lead to working "smarter."

If you approach your housecleaning with a professional attitude, you will try out different ideas until you learn to clean your house or apartment as efficiently as possible, taking all the shortcuts you can find. You may want to do a little of the work each day to free your weekends. Use your imagination and good sense.

ELIMINATE UNNECESSARY TASKS.

Consider the job. What do you really have to do? Simplify as much as you can. That means streamlining your house, your desk, your garage, your office. Streamlining requires the discipline to throw away what you do not need. We shall talk more about this when we talk about getting rid of clutter.

Remember. What you do not have you do not have to take care of. You do not have to feed it, repair it, dust it, wind it, store it, clean it. Less is better. Make your house functional and easy to maintain.

Here are some suggestions for eliminating unnecessary work in the house:

Buy washable no-iron curtains, clothing, sheets, table linens, and bedspreads. Fold and hang clothes immediately after the dryer shuts off. Dampen clothes to be ironed by putting in a wet towel with the load to be dampened and placing all in the dryer for fifteen to twenty minutes.

Whenever possible, buy home furnishings that have easy-care features. Products that resist dust, fingerprint smears, dulling, and stains help reduce housecleaning time. Non-stick pots and pans eliminate scouring. No-polish ceramic or synthetic hard floor coverings are a breeze to clean. So is washable carpet. A multicolored braided rug in the kitchen does not show dirt quickly and is easy to clean.

Use good wood cleaner and wax on your furniture twice a year. Never wax oftener. You can buff a good wax with felt or flannel. Spray the inside of your clean oven with a spray that helps prevent hardening of spatters. If you can afford it, buy a self-cleaning oven. Ask yourself if it is really necessary to vacuum more often than once a week.

Educate the family to eat in the kitchen, not all over the house. Encourage them to put things away, instead of laying them down. Members of the family must pick up after themselves. Anyone old enough to make a sandwich is old enough to clean up his own mess. The same holds true for project messes.

Remember the old adage "A stitch in time saves nine." Do what you should do when you should do it. Do dishes while food is easy to remove. Vacuum the furniture and rugs before the dirt is ground in. Wipe up spills promptly. Use resting-spoon holders at the preparation and cooking centers. Wipe up the counters and stove top as you work. A couple of sponges, one for the counter and one for the floor, work well for this purpose.

Put a little water in the bottom of your broiler pan the next time you broil something. The drippings are easy to remove, and it cuts down on smoke, too. Keep the sifter in a plastic bag to catch surplus flour. Put a piece of foil under pies that may spill over. Wipe off the rims of bottles before returning them to the refrigerator or cupboard. Use roasting bags or line pans with aluminum foil to cut down on scouring. Use bark in the garden to keep the weeds down.

When possible, save pot washing by preparing a complete meal in one pan or in the slow cooker, fondue pot, or electric skillet. Measure dry ingredients before liquids so you will not have to wash measuring spoons or cups twice.

Have ingredients, tools, and equipment conveniently arranged. Assemble ingredients before beginning to cook or bake.

Save unnecessary steps by using trays to carry more than two drinks or for clearing the dining room table of dishes. Put TV trays next to the refrigerator when cleaning it. Stack contents of refrigerator on trays. Use them when cleaning out drawers, cabinets, and closets, too.

Spray all-purpose, anti-grease cleanser on sink, tub, toilet, kitchen counter, and appliances as you enter each room to clean it. The cleanser can work for you while you pick up and empty trash.

Lay an old beach towel in the bottom of your bathtub and fill the tub with water, a little ammonia, and detergent. Soak stove racks in the tub while cleaning the oven. When you finish, use a brush to wipe them off.

Keep handy an ongoing shopping list where anyone in the family can jot down items you have run out of. Do your shopping once a week. Stock up on everything you can buy at one time. Plan your driving so that one trip takes care of several errands.

Do not handle mail oftener than you need to. Junk mail can be discarded without being opened. Pay bills once or twice a month, not as they come in.

These suggestions will help you start thinking of other time-saving ideas that you can add to the list. Do not be a slave to the house.

USE THE BEST TOOLS, APPLIANCES, AND CLEANERS AVAILABLE.

This does not mean a special cleaner for every job. Again, simpler is better.

Here are some suggestions from Kathie concerning tools and equipment:

I like having baskets to pile my stuff into while I clean a room. A lightweight hand vacuum is easy to use for fast pickups. I store small accessories in a shoe bag.

In the kitchen I like modern, time-saving appliances: a combination large mixer and bread maker, a self-cleaning range, a microwave oven, and a wheat grinder with stones.

I use rubber gloves whenever I clean. For longer wear I put

adhesive tape in the fingertips. I run cold water over the gloves before removing them.

Here is what I use to clean: sponges (I cut the corners off of the ones I use on the floor), a one-inch-wide paint brush for cleaning picture frames, diapers (six for windows—six for other cleaning jobs), a window squeegee, three pocket-aprons, a fold-up step stool, several brooms (one small one I cover with a rag and use in the ceiling corners), and a round-tipped nylon bristle hairbrush instead of a whisk broom.

Ammonia cleans the oven and makes glass sparkle. I keep a big jar of borax with a measuring cup inside on the bathroom counter. I use one-half cup twice a week to keep the toilet bowl clean. I keep a small container of liquid dishwashing soap in the bath room for hand washing. For woodwork, mix with a little ammonia. Rubbing alcohol shines bathroom fixtures, takes hair spray off mirrors, and is good for shining chrome. Other things I use: degreaser, powdered cleanser, furniture polish (oil), vinegar and water to clean windows, silver cleaner, and baking soda to wipe out the refrigerator and Teflon pan.

ORGANIZE WITH COLOR.

Give your imagination full rein when thinking of ways to use color. You will find a variety of supplies available in color: adhesive tape, thread, index cards, stickers, clothing, bedding, linens and towels, file tabs, and much more. You can buy tiny bottles of quick drying enamel paint in sixteen to twenty different colors.

You might begin by assigning a color to each member of the family. It should be his favorite. Identify each person's possessions with his color. Green sheets belong to Jim, blue ones to Mary Jo, and so on. Color code messages on the family calendar. Write Jim's dental appointments with green, Mary Jo's with blue.

Here are more ideas to help you start a new color life in your family. Use color to identify family articles such as toothbrushes and plastic drinking glasses; hair brushes and combs; shower caps and roller bags; bathrobes, pajamas, and slippers; socks; dishpans that hold clean clothes to be put away; dishpans or bins for each child's toys; toy bags for different toys or different people; towels and wash cloths.

Use colored index cards. Regular recipes go on white cards, low calorie recipes on colored cards. For identifying storage boxes use yellow cards for hobby supplies, green for kitchen extras, orange for holiday supplies, blue for miscellaneous items.

When moving, color code the rooms and boxes. Mark the kitchen boxes with a piece of colored tape. Then make the floor plan of the kitchen the same color. Hang the floor plan in an easy-to-spot location for movers to see. Tie yarn around handles or chair legs to match the color of the room the furniture goes in.

Color code tools for inside and outside use. Mark outside gas and water shutoffs with color. Use color to mark keys. One color for the house key, another for the garage, and so on.

Color code special events on the calendar. Circle paydays with green, birthdays with red.

Mark children's rain boots, lunch pails, and coats with colored tape. Color code containers for sorting the wash. Put colored tape around the neck of hangers to color code them to the person whose clothes are to be hung on them. Use a wild-colored adhesive tape on hangers to hang clothes that need mending.

If two children share a room and closet, paint the inside of the closet one color on one side and another color on the other side.

Color code sponges. Each room can have a color; bathroom blue, kitchen green, or all floor sponges pink. When washing windows, color code sponges to buckets; one color for soapy water, the other for rinse water.

Use different colored stickers on large brown envelopes to identify charge accounts, bank accounts, credit cards, and medical bills. Put the labels on the top edge of the envelopes so that when all are lined up in a lidless box, the colors show at a glance. List the numbers and names of each account on the front of the envelopes.

As you can see, there are many ways to put color in your life. Some of them might work well in your family. Others will not.

Experiment with color, and you will have an easy, fun-to-use way to organize and save more time.

MAKE THE TELEPHONE AN ALLY

Does anyone in your family think that he would have a better chance of getting your full attention if he went to the neighbors' and called you on the telephone?

If you ever allow the telephone to rob you of valuable time that could be used more profitably, try this. For one week, record the amount of time you spend talking on the telephone. Also write down with whom and about what you talk. This will give you some idea as to how you spend telephone time. The telephone can be a very useful tool if you use it wisely. It can save time instead of robbing you of it.

Let your telephone do your running around for you. Use it to inquire about the availability of supplies, compare prices, and delegate tasks. You can eliminate many miles of driving and even a great deal of letter writing if you learn to use your telephone effectively.

Under certain circumstances, you may want to ignore its ringing. How many times have you been leaving the house on the way to keep an appointment when the telephone rang? Do you always go back and answer it? If so, you may find the minutes ticking away, making it impossible for you to get where you were going on time. How much better if you can resist the temptation to answer the phone at times like that!

Do not feel obligated to submit to a demanding ring when you are in the middle of an important task. If the call is urgent, the caller will call again. If you think it might be an emergency, answer. But if it is not, tell your caller you are busy at the moment, and you will return the call at four o'clock or whatever time suits your schedule.

Make the telephone an ally by clustering your telephoning at one time of the day, perhaps at lunchtime or in the late afternoon. Let your friends know what time you like to receive calls.

It is also important to learn to end conversations that may go on and on. Do not be afraid of offending the caller when you seem brief or busy. You *are* busy, so tell your caller that you are. Keep a supply of postcards on hand for brief replies. This will eliminate some time-consuming telephone calls. Enclose postcards when you need a reply, too.

Save the fun calls to friends for a reward for getting priority tasks finished in prime time. Then be sure you are not infringing on your friend's time before you settle down for a lengthy chat.

The telephone should be the focal point of your message center, an area every family needs. What your message center will be like depends on your house and your family. You can adapt ideas given here to your own situation. Our message center, for example, differs from that of the Lidens.

Our family calendar hangs on the wall above the telephone. We use the side of the cupboard for important phone numbers. On a nail under the calendar we attach sheets of paper containing information about current happenings such as notes from school, the school menu, a list of the names of the women in my Bible study, et cetera. On the kitchen counter we keep our telephone message book, the ongoing shopping list, a decorated can full of sharpened pencils and a large see-through plastic canister containing the many little items we often need such as rubber bands, small stapler, glue, labels, paper clips, Scotch tape, and so on. We store the city telephone book, church directory, and frequently called numbers in a cupboard under the telephone.

The Lidens have framed a bulletin board in their message center. They use an oversized calendar with plenty of writing space. In the right hand corner they write important dates: birthdays, anniversaries, special holidays. Paydays are circled in green. Birthdays and other special days are circled in red.

For small children who cannot read or who just love the excitement of holidays, you could buy some gummed holiday, special event, or gold star stickers. On the Sunday squares put some special stickers of drawings of a church or Christ.

Every morning during breakfast at the Liden house each person uses his own colored pencil, which hangs by a string on the bulletin board, to initial the calendar space for the day. This is a reminder of appointments, for example, and school and job take-alongs.

Also posted on the bulletin board is the menu for the week. Whoever gets home first can begin dinner. By looking at the menu the family can also see which night might be a good one to ask some friends to stop by and share dinner.

Remember that little things can cause the greatest time loss. How often have you wasted time looking for a pencil? Every September when school supplies go on special you can buy a dozen pencils for very little money. Have a central place, like our can beside the telephone, in which to keep them. Then, whenever you see a pencil on the floor or lying elsewhere around the house, return it to the can. There will always be an ample supply of pencils, and you will never again waste time looking for one.

The telephone message notebook has been especially helpful. Every telephone message is recorded under the day's date in a spiral notebook. Each of us has learned to ask the caller for his name when we take a call. No longer do we have bits and pieces of paper with the telephone numbers and notes scribbled on them. When anyone returns home, the first thing he does is check the book to see if there were any calls for him while he was gone.

We use the message book to check on long distance calls, to look up information we have forgotten, to verify the date of a call, and so on. I highly recommend using such a book.

Basically, the message center will include the family calendar, shopping list, message book, telephone numbers in several forms including a personal "Yellow Pages" put together by you, pencils, and whatever else you want to add.

Other things you might want to keep in your message center are: an emergency phone list, repair lists, help lists, reminders, hooks for keys, and a master list for storage boxes.

A family operation manual is extremely valuable if you ever have to be away. This will contain routine information about your day-to-day living: garbage pickup day, watering times, care of pets, and the like.

With all the good-looking wall baskets available, why not tack one next to your message center to hold a family file? Label a file folder for each member of the family. Staple a couple of blank pieces of paper to the inside of the folder for jotting down information. The top page should include dates of shots and any allergy to drugs, birthday, driver's license number, social security number, and so on. Inside the folder put the notes the children bring home from school or Sunday school, recreation notices, camp applications, and any other information that applies to the individual.

A well-organized message center and good telephone habits will create many more minutes for you to do the things you really want to do.

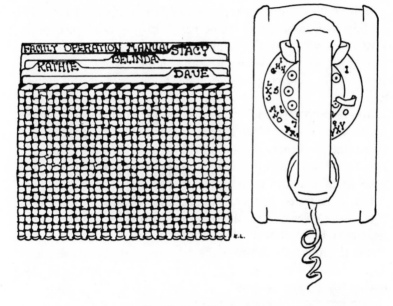

GET RID OF CLUTTER

You can learn to say no, make the minute work for you, work "smarter," and make the telephone your ally, yet still have a messy-looking house. Why? Probably because of all the clutter.

Perhaps this book has motivated you to reorganize your house to make it more functional, and you have determined that this time things are going to be different. Everyone will put his things away, not down. There will be no eating on foot. Coats and sweaters will be hung up. Everyone will leave the bathroom tidy.

It may work for a while, but clutter, public enemy number one, has a casual way of sneaking up. Little things begin to turn up far from their proper places. Mail gets put on the mantle. Magazines and newspapers are thrown on a chair or on the floor. Someone ignores the telephone message book and scribbles an important message on the edge of a department store flyer. Pencils are scattered around the house. You find the hand towel on the bathroom floor and clean clothes piled on a chair. Empty jars line the kitchen counter.

Believe it or not, a few ground rules and some nifty ideas for dealing with troublesome items can help you establish control. That old saying "A place for everything and everything in its place" is basic, but to make it work you must take it further than you may think at first glance. You must provide places for clutter, too.

You need to view each room looking for trouble spots. Divide the room into areas. Identify the problems. Try to decide what causes the problems. You will probably find that most of them fit into one of two categories: space or paper. The next step is to find ways to gain control in those two areas.

Let us begin by conquering space. Streamline each room of your house. Never leave anything out that does not add to the decorative or functional scheme of the room. Unnecessary items clutter the room, detract from the attractiveness, and gather dust. Many houses contain great quantities of permanent clutter. Do not let this happen to you.

Another old adage about throwing away everything not used for a year is a good rule to follow. Tackle one small area of the house at a time. Use three boxes, one for throwaways, one for give-aways, and one for things to arrange later in storage. Be ruthless. Get rid of everything that takes precious space, but does not pay its way.

One woman says that she finds it easy to cut down on clutter when she pretends she is moving into a house half the size of the one in which she lives. Another woman pretends someone else is going through her things after her death. This helps her to see what has value and what does not.

Once you have rid yourself of unnecessary clutter, keep it from accumulating again by periodically scheduling a Discard Day on family night. On that day let everyone in the family go through his own things and get rid of items he has not used in a long time. If he cannot part with something, put it in a labeled storage box.

Now, take a look at the house and see which things are still cluttering. With a little ingenuity.you can provide places for these stubborn, troublesome items.

Put baskets in each room to hold current newspapers, magazines, books, and other frequently used items. One family uses wicker baskets nailed to the wall over each person's coat hook in the back hallway to store winter caps, gloves, and scarves. Rolled-up newspapers or magazines can also go in attractive wine racks attached to a living or family room wall.

Make use of clutter shelves, drawers, and closets. We have a drawer in our kitchen that we reserve for clutter. We frequently clean out this drawer to make room for clutter we are sure to have in a hurried moment.

Each of our children has a clutter drawer or space in his or her bedroom. Providing such a space eliminates the need to throw things down on a bed or desk. Various size boxes fill Carla's clutter drawer, a long one in her chest of drawers. Since she is a very organized little girl, she likes to be able to sort clutter in this way even when she is pressed for time.

Eric's clutter spot is a large box on one of his closet shelves. A clean room is not high on his priority list, so he uses his clutter shelf less effectively than Carla, often forgetting to empty it when he has time. Still, it helps him keep his room in better shape than he would without it.

The Lidens have a clutter closet about which we talked in chapter 3. They also have used a trunk for sports equipment in the entrance hall, and wicker baskets for clutter in every room of the house. Kathie also uses these baskets to clear the room while cleaning.

Treasure chests can solve a lot of clutter problems, too. For Christmas one year, Dave's father made each of the Liden girls a treasure chest with a lock. They hold their treasures; what else? Things like autograph books, photographs, special letters, awards, and souvenirs of all kinds.

To bring under control the second category of clutter, paper, also requires some thought and imagination. Most of your paper problem will be solved if you establish a home office. This office can be as simple or as fancy as you want to make it. It should have a desk or table, some kind of filing system, basic writing supplies (pencils, pens, stamps, paper), and a wastebasket.

A friend of the Lidens has come up with an ingenious idea for a clutter center in the home office (see drawing). You can adapt this idea to small shoe boxes, baskets, or wooden or plastic boxes.

Did you know that the masses of paper cluttering your home and office fall into one of three categories? A piece of paper is something to be discarded, something that requires a response, or something with information that you need to keep.

Nearly all time management experts advise handling paper only once. To do this, you must condition yourself to sort immediately any paper that comes to you. After throwing away the junk, try to respond to the paper in the second category right away. If you cannot, make a note on the paper and put it in a To Do file. The third group goes in the file folder in which it belongs.

If you do not have a filing system, invest in some inexpensive manila file folders and get a cardboard box to put them in. Label them as broadly as possible. You might have folders for insurance, medical records, money, car, and purchases (warranties, instructions, etc.).

Magazines fall into a special category. "I would be tarred and feathered if I ever advised friends to toss out their magazines after two months," says Kathie. "I have some interior decorating books that go back twenty years."

This is what Kathie does. As soon as she buys a magazine, she staples a three-by-five-inch card inside the cover. As she reads the magazine, she writes on the card the numbers of the pages she wants to save. She keeps the two most recent issues on a table or in a basket in the living room. When the time comes to discard the magazine, she uses her handy X-acto knife to zip down the pages. She stores the articles in standard three-ring notebooks under the appropriate headings. (She has a three-hole punch.)

"If I really want a good book to read, I read my notebooks," Kathie says, laughing. "When I get tired of an article, I throw it out."

You can also store magazines by standing them upright in a box. Store a year's issues and label the box. Many libraries store magazines this way.

What about children and paper? The two go together, right? To handle the daily intake of children's papers, provide a box or dishpan for them in each child's room. Teach your child to go through the box periodically and discard what he no longer needs. His best works can go into his treasure chest or into his personal file. Remember to select some of his papers to pin to the family bulletin board.

When the Liden girls were in junior high school, their parents gave them dishpans with manila folders. They taught the girls how to label their folders and file papers.

When the girls reached high school, Kathie bought them each a cardboard box that has hanging folders. These are very easy to use. Now they have a section for their bank books, checks, social security cards, birth certificates, photographs they have not put in their albums, letters, and so on.

To help your children keep a brief record of the years they are growing up, each year make up a sheet of vital information. Title it "Third Grade," "Fourth Grade," or whatever. Record the name of the child's teacher, honors received, immunization record, height and weight, address, best friends, and his school picture for that year. Also have a place for his signature. Children love reminiscing by going through photograph albums, scrapbooks, and records.

Now we come to the last bit of advice about keeping clutter to a minimum. Become a "picker upper" and teach your family the picking-up habit.

Schedule pickup times: in the late afternoon, before going to bed, before leaving the house in the morning, whatever works best for your family. Incorporate into the family the Scout rule "Leave an area better than you found it." Teach every family member responsibility for cleaning up after himself wherever he is.

Be practical. Be patient. Persevere. Clutter will rear its ugly head from time to time, but with practice things will stay in place more often than they will stray.

Recognize the fact that time is life. Follow the principles of time management, adding prayer to the list. Say yes only to activities that fit your goals and your time schedule. Make the minute work for you. Work "smarter." Make the telephone an ally. Get rid of clutter. By doing these things you will gain control of the things you have to do. By managing the minute you will have time for your family and for the things you want to do. What a beautiful reward for managing time wisely!

5

Set Up Workable
Time Plans

You will find the key to good management by answering the question When do we do what? To answer that question in business, executives set up a schedule, or work plan. To run a home efficiently, you need to do the same thing.

A good schedule sets you free. It can help you see the way you are doing your work and also help you to analyze and improve what you are doing so that you can get more done in less time. A schedule will put you in charge of what you do rather than having what you do in charge of you.

The trick to mastering a schedule is to stay in complete control. Think of the schedule as a handrail provided when you must climb a flight of stairs. When you need it, you can reach out and hang on. When you do not need it, you can let go. It is simply a guide provided to steady you and aid your progress.

It is unbelievably easy to set up a workable schedule for each member of the family. This can be done on family night if you wish. Divide a piece of paper into seven spaces for the seven days of the week. Label the time blocks of activities in which you are now involved, for example:

Sunday: 8:30—11:00 church
Tuesday: 6:00—9:00 night class

Budget your days loosely. Allow large chunks of time to avoid the frustration of overscheduling. Group phone calls. Fill in the hours for appointments. Assign blocks of time for projects.

Look over the chart. Question each entry. Have you picked the best times to do your tasks? Can some of them be eliminated? Can you consolidate some of the tasks, for example, cook two meals at one time? Are you too meticulous? Does your schedule include things you really want to do, such as read a particular book or work on a piece of stitchery? Does it reflect your goals and values?

The schedule is your guide. If you make it too detailed, you will soon abandon it, because a complicated guide is too much trouble. A simple schedule will give direction to your life and help you focus on completion of as many high priority items as you can each day.

In planning your schedule, practice the principles of effective time management outlined in chapter 4. Rank jobs as to their importance and urgency. Do first things first. Take time in the evening to plan the next day. Run through your mind what must be done and decide on the first thing you will do.

You will have routine tasks every day. If you can take fifteen to thirty minutes each morning to do things such as make the beds, straighten up the kitchen, tidy the house, or see that these tasks are done, it will free you for the other more important tasks of the day.

I find it a great help to establish time patterns. I do my writing in the library nearly every day from 10:00 until 3:00. That gives me early morning time to get any chores done at home. I leave the house in good order. On my best days I have dinner in the slow cooker and everything set up to facilitate having dinner ready soon after the whole family gets home.

Obviously, if I must go to one of the children's schools for a conference or take someone to the doctor or dentist, I have to change my schedule. Give yourself room for the unexpected. You can do what you want to with your schedule, but follow it whenever it is possible and practical.

The chores on your schedule should have a starting and stopping place. If you plan to do spring housecleaning, for example, do no more than one room a day. Establish a quitting time and stick to it.

Your schedule should also include rest periods and times for meditation and prayer. This will insure time for the joys and blessings of the present. We need to take time to look, to feel, and to care. We need a time to dream, to sit in the sun, and to let the earth sift through our fingers.

Each of you should make room on your schedule for other members of the family. Paul Jongeward, a busy Christian psychologist, includes his family's plans on his own schedule. He can see at a glance what each family member is doing at any hour of the day. He stays actively involved in their lives, praying for specific activities as they come up.

What a wonderful way to keep track of the family! Such a superb manager should have little difficulty keeping things running smoothly and profitably. Mastering a time schedule may be a little tricky at first, but do not give up. The family that runs smoothly does so because the members involved have mapped out a sequence of operations that will accomplish all work objectives. The better you can learn to do this, the more effective your family will become.

How to Make Your Own Priority Notebook

Thousands of people have learned the effectiveness of gathering the bits and pieces of valuable information and records they use and putting them in one place. This one source book—the priority notebook—serves all functions. This simple yet comprehensive book should fit your pocket or purse. It is a pocket-size "office."

Your priority notebook must be tailor-made to your own special needs and interests. Rose Kennedy used hers to jot down anything she wanted to remember. Her notebook contained useful facts and ideas and quotations.

The president of a large Portland bank calls his notebook "my brains." In his notebook he keeps a telephone log, schedule for the week, goals, a To Do list, plans for the weekend, financial information, Bible verses to read when he feels uptight, measurements for a building project, expenses of the day, a list of books to read, and a few checks and business cards.

Anne Ortlund, author and musician, divides her notebook into six sections. First comes the calendar, which has a page for each day. The name of the day and the date are written at the top. She keeps three months scheduled in her notebook. As she reaches the end of the day, she evaluates the tasks left unfinished. Some she reschedules. Others she eliminates. Then she throws the page away.

Anne lists her goals in the next section. The third section contains her current Bible study on which she makes daily notes in the notebook. In section four she keeps the names of those she is discipling. She makes notes about what they are studying, their prayer needs, and so on. Section five contains notes on sermons she hears, and the last section is for prayers.[1]

Your notebook should include all information you must have at your fingertips. The ideal notebook is looseleaf so that you can take out sections you do not need at the moment and store them in a file box until you need to reinsert them in the notebook.

Choose the size notebook that suits you best. It should be small enough to fit into your purse or pocket, but large enough to hold postcards and checks. Most people like the 7-by-4½-inch size. This one uses paper 6¾-by-3¾ inches. Dave Liden uses the 7-by-4½-inch size, but he also has a 4½-by-3-inch notebook with its own pencil, which slips into the pocket of his larger notebook. Whenever his clothes do not have a pocket large enough for his bigger notebook, he slips the smaller one into his shirt pocket.

You can buy notebooks at any office supply or stationery store.

You can buy plain sheets, lined sheets, sheets for expenses, appointment sheets, activities sheets, and time records. Discount and variety stores also carry notebooks at very low cost. These inexpensive ones do not have pockets. Kathie uses them to store overflow material from her priority notebook.

After you have chosen your notebook, buy index dividers. These will have clear tabs into which you slide the index labels. Also buy a calendar that shows the month at a glance and will easily slip into the pocket of your notebook.

Circle in red the important dates—anniversaries, birthdays, et cetera. Next, pencil in appointments, meetings, and other scheduled events. You can easily erase penciled notations to make changes.

Now you must organize the notebook. If you use numbered tabs, list the numbers on the first divider. You can create a plain divider page by cutting the number off the ones you do not need. This first page may have the sections listed with a personal memoranda (see illustration).

You might want to include additional information on your personal memoranda page or pages:

Emergency phone numbers:
- sheriff
- doctors
- ambulance
- fire
- dentist
- hospital

Names or numbers of:
- lawyer
- accountant
- babysitter
- minister
- library
- cleaners
- gas station

Notebook Sections

1. Family
2. Money
3. Ideas and notes
4. Projects to do
5. Job and other
   responsibilities

Personal Memoranda

This book belongs to:

name _____

address _____

_____

phone _____

business _____

address _____

_____

phone _____ ext. ____

social security no. _____

drivers license no. _____

doctor _____

phone _____

blood type _____

allergies _____

emergency numbers:

ambulance _____

fire _____

police _____

in case of emergency notify:

_____

_____

DESIGNED BY KATHIE LIDEN

1

2

3

4

5

- friends or neighbors
- druggist
- insurance agents
- beauty shop
- post office
- garage

Family:
- children
    school—grade—teacher—telephone
- parents
    name—address—telephone
- sisters and brothers

Finance:
- bank account numbers
- credit card record
- list of insurance policies and their numbers

Cars:
- make—model
- license number
- registration number
- insurance company, policy number, agent

Kathie titled the first section in her notebook "Family, Friends, and the Lord." This section contains important information about her family, including social security numbers, driver's license numbers, business address and telephone numbers, gift ideas, sizes, close friends, blood type, and much more. She also mounts a photograph of the person on the back of his/her information sheet.

On information sheets about friends, you may include dates you have them for dinner and what you served. You may also record any special likes and dislikes.

Kathie used "P" as a subsection on prayer. She drew vertical lines through the pages in this section. The left half of each page is titled "Requests" and the right half "Answers."

The second subtitle in this section is "B" for Bible. This section contains Bible verses, which Kathie changes from time to time. She also has ongoing Bible study projects.

"Section one, 'Family, Friends and the Lord,' is my first priority," says Kathie. "Every morning before starting any activities, I review this section."

The second section in Kathie's notebook has a checklist and a weekly schedule. She lists goals on the page opposite the schedule.

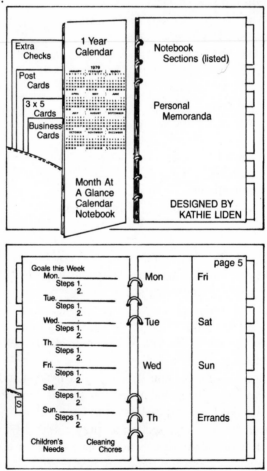

Additional pages in this section may include family requests to think over, family problems to discuss, and family night activities. Under days of the week, you may list dinner menus, calls to make, letters to write.

"I review this section and the monthly calendar every evening," says Kathie. "From these notes I make out a To Do list. I clip this list to the front of my notebook or to the refrigerator. It is important to keep the list in sight."

Kathie's notebook also contains: section three: Shopping, Food, Money; section four: Quotes, Art, Decorating, Yard; section five: Beauty, Clothes, Sewing; section 6: Books, Tapes, Notes; section 7: Business; section 8: Addresses, Telephone numbers, Records.

"Many of these sections in my notebook overflow," Kathie says, "so I have extra notebooks on my desk to contain the excess."

The overflow includes: Housekeeping (ideas, tips, formulas); Holidays and Special Days (Christmas mailing list, gift lists, projects to do); Quotes, Drawings, and Ideas for Decorating; Bible Study Projects; Other Study Projects; Business; Travel (camping lists, supplies, places to visit); Health, Diet, and Exercises.

Kathie can take any of these sections and insert them in her priority notebook when she needs them.

The following are suggestions of items you might want to include in your own notebook. Choose only what suits your needs and interests.

- Personal memoranda
- House directory
- Calendar with appointments and birthdays marked
- Monthly and weekly schedule
- Responsibilities
- Goals and plans
- Housekeeping schedule
- To Do list (colored page)

- Master list of A's (important things to do) and B's (things you would like to do)
- A Don't Forget list
- Errands list
- Special cleaning in house and yard
- Letters (sent and received list)
- Records of membership and dues to groups and organizations
- Gift ideas
- Color swatches of fabrics for sewing clothes and home decorating
- Samples of yardage from rooms in the house
- Swatches of carpet. Popsicle sticks painted with wall paint or furniture paint. Samples of wallpaper.
- Measurements of furniture, windows, and rooms
- Clothes sizes and preferences
- Garden calendar
- Wish list of books to purchase and code numbers of your favorite library books
- List of items to buy (needs and wants)
- Master list for grocery shopping
- Income tax deductions
- Allowances for children
- Master shopping lists
- Household budget plans and goals for balancing the budget
- Bargains of the month—sales
- Magazines ordered
- Sermon notes
- Ideas you want to discuss with your spouse or children
- Study guides
- Family night ideas
- Quotes to inspire you
- How to remove common stains
- Basic first-aid instructions
- Ideas for running the house
- Problems you need to deal with
- Emergency information

- Metrics conversion chart
- Repair list
- Places of interest you may want to visit
- Prayer requests
- Notes about hobbies—addresses to obtain inspiration and supplies
- Car records—dates of last tune-up, when you bought your tires, when you changed oil, and so on
- Business goals and how to achieve them
- Shortcuts in cooking—a recipe from a friend or TV program
- Menu for the week
- Record of what you serve company for dinner
- Calorie counter
- List of supplies for camping and mini-trips
- Ideas for Christmas
- Exercise guide
- Health records: shots, physical checkups
- Favorite beauty products
- Cute sayings of children
- Three-by-five-inch cards
- Address book
- Business cards
- Ruler on paper
- Checkbook
- Extra keys
- Coupons you plan to use
- Dates—last haircut, when you stripped the bed, and so on

A few guidelines will help you decide what to include in your priority notebook.

MAKE IT MULTIPURPOSE.

Keep everything in one place. Scattered duplication of records causes confusion and frustration.

MAKE IT PERSONAL.

Include only the information you need and will use.

KEEP IT CONVENIENT.

Your planner notebook should always be at your fingertips, ready to use. Make it part of your habit system. When an idea strikes, instead of reaching for a scrap of paper, reach for your notebook. If you do not use it, you have created a useless pocket or purse stuffer, nothing more.

MAKE IT ORDERLY.

Set up your sections first. Fit the information into the proper section. As a rule of thumb, schedule and organize similar tasks and information together.

If you are willing to invest a little time in setting up a priority notebook, you will reap a tremendous bonus in time. You will also avoid costly errors, backtracking, and doing things over. Remember, without investment, there will be no benefits.

6

Raise Responsible Children

Nothing challenges the marital partnership more than the arrival of children. The father and mother must pool their resources to meet the problems sure to come up as they train a child for adulthood. This task involves more than physical care and discipline. It also involves helping the child grow into a confident individual with his own unique ideas and behavior, ready to find God's plan for his life.

Much of what your children learn will be determined by what you model. You have no choice. You cannot escape the truth—children do what you do, not what you say. Attitudes are caught, not taught.

It does not matter whether you are teaching your children about God, how to manage money, or how to be a productive person. The same truth applies. We communicate through our attitudes, what we do, and how we do it much more clearly than we communicate through words. We are often inconsistent and hypocritical.

We punish the petty dishonesty of our children—and tell the

bus driver they are still "half fare." We tell our children to eat in the kitchen, whereas we eat in the living room in front of the television set. We tell them to put their toys away, and they see Daddy's new shovel rusting in the yard.

Many times the difference between our words and our actions communicates that there is one set of rules for children and a different set for parents. Actually, parents are nothing more than grown-up children. They share with their children the ability to think, feel, make decisions, and form values. This common human bond ties parents and children together in their need for help and understanding in Christian love.

The problem comes in our interpretation of what it means to model Christianity. People who think being a Christian means being good, will certainly back away from modeling the Christian faith. Jesus told us that no one is good except God. So relax.

Christianity is not being good. Christianity is a *relationship* with Jesus Christ. To try to stay on a pedestal denies that bond of humanity you have with your children and makes it extremely difficult to relate to them. They should see your relationship with Jesus and transformation taking place as you constantly bring Him into your life to help you with the struggles you have. As you grow, they will see joy, freedom, kindness, self-control, and a measure of peace, something they too will experience as their own lives begin the process of transformation. We are learners together.

Your children get angry. So do you. It is how you handle your anger that is important. If you can direct your anger at an action, not at a person, perhaps you can help your children to direct their anger correctly too.

Instead of yelling at his brother, "You pig! You always snoop in other people's things. I hate you!" a child can learn to say, "I hate it when people come into my room without my permission. It makes me very, very angry!"

Do not fool yourself. Your children *can* see your humanity, so enjoy the freedom that fact brings. Be real. When children hear parents confess a fault, they will learn to confess theirs, also.

Children need to know that we have the same feelings, weaknesses, and temptations they have. Some children think it is easy for fathers and mothers to be good, because they never see any of their parents' struggles.

"Fathers, especially, need to show their humanness," said Dr. Theodore Isaac Ruben, well-known psychiatrist, appearing as a guest on the "Phil Donahue Show." "A child should know his father is capable of tears."

What is your attitude toward life? Are you full of hope and trust in God? To many of us, the problems of our times seem so monumental that instead of communicating a positive, hopeful attitude to our children, we communicate despair. Such communication will sabotage your effort to raise individuals who look with hope to the future.

What are your attitudes toward order, organization, and work? If you want to teach a child to put his room in order before going to bed at night and to lay out clothes for the next morning, you must do those things yourself. Never assign to your children tasks that you would not do yourself. In fact, a very good way to get cooperation on chores is to be first to volunteer for the less popular jobs.

Start Early to Build Good Habits

Did you know that at as early as one month, a baby recognizes his mother's voice and can connect it to her face? At three months a baby knows whether his mother is talking to him or to someone else.

Most of us underestimate our children's readiness for training. Minutes well spent now will save hours later. A few minutes training a two-year-old may save hours of scolding a twelve-year-old. Habits form character.

Children sometimes play the game "Teach Me, If You Can Catch Me." Many parents complain that when their children want to help, they cannot, and when they are old enough, they will not. Catch them when they are willing, even if it means taking extra time to help them learn how to complete a task. Do not discourage them because you think they are too young, too slow, and too messy.

Responsibility begins with learning to take care of personal needs and belongings. No one else should do work for someone who can be doing it himself. After a child reaches school age, his week can be divided somewhat like this:

$$
\begin{array}{rl}
38 & \text{hours at school} \\
4 & \text{hours at church} \\
\underline{70} & \text{hours sleeping} \\
112 & \text{hours total}
\end{array}
$$

$$
\begin{array}{rl}
168 & \text{total hours in a week} \\
\underline{-112} & \\
56 & \text{hours in home environment}
\end{array}
$$

Home becomes an apprentice shop where children spend most of their time. By the time he is fourteen or fifteen, a child should be able to do everything necessary to run a home. No one will take the time to train your child the way you can. You must prepare your children to stand on their own two feet, to become the best of whatever they are.

The Bible advises: "Train up a child in the way he should go [and in keeping with his individual gift or bent], and when he is old he will not depart from it" (Proverbs 22:6, Amp.*).

It is extremely important to see our children as individuals having their own interests and aptitudes and not as mere replicas of ourselves or of each other. Each child has his own combination of inborn traits that affect his interests, dreams, ambitions, and behavior. To give him proper training and guidance, we must know who he is at different stages of his life.

---

* *The Amplified Bible.*

MAKE WORK EASY AND VARIED

Remember five things when teaching work skills to children. FIRST, SHOW CHILDREN HOW TO DO EACH NEW JOB, SET GUIDELINES, AND INSPECT WHAT THEY HAVE DONE.

Never assume the child knows how to do something if he has never seen you demonstrate it. He may even think he knows how.

Young children will benefit from visual aids. To teach a child how to set the table correctly, use a large sheet of construction paper. Glue to it a paper plate, paper cup (glass), napkin, plastic fork, spoon, and knife. Tack it to the bulletin board where the youngster can refer to it from time to time.

Do not expect perfection from your children, but do inspect for reasonable effort and skill. Let them know when they have done a good job. Do not be critical, but tactfully show the child ways to improve if his effort was truly unsatisfactory.

SECOND, EQUIP YOUR HOUSE FOR CHILDREN.

Rods should be low enough for children to reach their own clothes. Dish shelves, too, should be accessible to children. Step stools, special towel racks, laundry hampers in each bedroom, color coding, clutter drawers, and closets are just a few of the things necessary for helping your child learn to help.

Begin when your children are babies to store their toys in toy

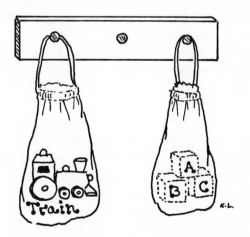

bags, dishpans, or small boxes. Each one will store a few toys. If a child is allowed to play with one bag, pan, or box at a time, he will have less to clean up. Toy bags can be hung in the child's closet and rotated. Every two months some of the bags may rotate to garage storage. These are the resting toys. If you use dishpans or boxes, resting toys go on the top shelf of the closet. Active toys stay on the lower shelf. See closet drawing in chapter 3.

Spend time organizing the bags for best efficiency. Three puzzles, for example, may be enough for one bag. Mark the backs of puzzle pieces with felt-tip pen, a different color for each puzzle. Label the bags, boxes, or pans so their contents can be quickly identified.

Think of all the ways you can equip your house for children. The effort will pay off. Children easily learn to help when they have equipment within their reach. They can work without constantly asking for Mother's or Father's help to get what they need.

THIRD, USE MEASUREMENTS OF TIME.

Have a starting and a stopping place. When Kathie's daughters were in their early teens, the Lidens spent two hours working as a family every Saturday morning. They knew they would be free at the end of the two hours.

"This worked beautifully for our family at that time," says Kathie. "To make it work you must fill the two hours. If you finish the housecleaning, you can bake, do yard work, or mending. Everyone knows he will work from 9:00 until 11:00, so he doesn't try to speed through to get done early. It's amazing how much four people can do in just two hours."

A fifteen-minute family work period every morning is practical for some. If there are three of you working, that is forty-five minutes of work done at a peak energy time of the day.

If you have young children, use the timer for five, ten, or fifteen-minute periods, or assign jobs by numbers. "You have two jobs this week."

You will get greater cooperation if children can see an end to the work. They can learn to plan their time realistically, which will bring them one step nearer maturity.

FOURTH, COLLECT A STOREHOUSE OF IDEAS.

Variety keeps work interesting and fun. A Saturday box, for example, may motivate children to put away their things for a while, but in time the novelty will wear off. A Saturday box is something a mother dreamed up when her children tuned out her constant reminders to put away sweaters, books, and toys. Anything left out at night went into the Saturday box to be redeemed on that day for a penny.

Most of us know that yelling at children is the least effective way of getting their help. "Yelling at my children to get them to do something," says one mother, "is like honking the horn to stop the car from rolling downhill."

Every parent should collect a number of ideas that will be effective. Here are a few:

Hand puppets. Give children hand puppets. The puppet, not the child, picks up the toys. Better still, have the children make the puppets to use.

Pretending games. The parent says, "I need a taxi (or truck)." The "taxi" or "truck" comes on hands and knees to carry the cargo or do the errand the parent wants done.

Imaginary friends. If your child has an imaginary friend, put him to work. The child loves to include him in his activities.

Numbers. Suggest, "I'll pick up ten things, and you pick up ten things."

Special occasions. Getting ready for Daddy's return from work, say, "Let's make this room a happy room before Daddy comes home."

Music box. Have children try to pick up toys before the music box stops playing its tune.

Timer. Set the timer for three minutes and try to pick up all the toys before the bell rings. Alter this by having the child decide how long the job will take. He can set the timer himself and see how close he can come to the time he chose.

Positions. Children can take turns with different house duties such as answering the telephone. Give each position a title. Tele-Talker, for example, might be the official telephone person. Other possible positions: Dust Deputy, Pet Caretaker, Washroom Patrol, and so on. You can make badges for the children to wear, if they like that sort of thing.

Treasures. Choose one picture or school paper a day to hang on the family bulletin board. On family night choose the best paper of the week to go in the child's treasure box, a special box in which he keeps special treasures. Remember to include papers on which he shows improvement as well as the papers in subjects in which he always excels.

Record keeping. Put grocery receipts into a jar on the kitchen counter. At the end of the month the child learning record-keeping for the family can total the receipts and report on what the family is spending at the grocery store.

Add ideas of your own. Having a storehouse of ideas will provide the variety that will keep work interesting and fun at your house.

FIFTH, HAVE A REGULAR PICK-UP TIME.

Spend five or ten minutes picking up clutter and clearing dressers and tabletops before major housecleaning chores begin. Other good pick-up times are in late afternoon, before going to bed, or in the morning before leaving the house. If you schedule regular pick-up times, the house will always look reasonably good and cleaning will be much easier.

GET COOPERATION BY USING CHORE CHARTS

Out of your family meeting will come many of the plans that keep the family running smoothly. For example, during family night at the Lawson home, the family discussed the family work load. They came up with ideas for dividing the work so that no one had to do more than his fair share. Out of this came their family chore charts.

You can plan a series of family nights on the theme "Working Together." Share with your family Proverbs 20:11. "Even a child is known by his doings, whether his work be pure, and whether it be right'' (KJV).

Conduct a family work party on one of these nights. Make an inventory of what has to be done to keep the house running smoothly. Ideally, father and mother should be included on chore charts and jobs rotated through the family. Sometimes this is not practical.

Before we set up our most recent chore chart, Everett went through the house with pencil and paper. Room by room he listed all the repair and upkeep jobs he felt he needed to do. He presented the three page list to the family. We all decided that Daddy should be excluded from our everyday chore chart so that he could be free to work on his repair list as he had time. I take my turn with the children at the chores as they rotate each week.

When setting up work assignments or work charts, keep in mind these basic points:

Consider the strength and age of each family member so as to avoid assignments that are either too easy or too difficult.

If practical, include parents. Parents can volunteer to begin with the least popular jobs. Example has always been the most effective way to teach skills. Remember, we cannot give our children something we do not have.

No one should be expected to do more than his share of the work. Make special allowances for family members who have a great deal of pressure and responsibility outside the home. Remember to show appreciation for one another's efforts.

Keep work charts very simple and clear. We will suggest chore ideas for children of different ages. Select only the ones that suit your family's needs.

Chore Ideas for Children

2-3-year-olds

It is better to have your child do *one* or *two* items consistently than to list a lot of jobs that rarely get daily attention.

Suggested Chores

Daily Before Breakfast

1. Undress (usually can).
2. Hang pajamas on low hook.
3. Dress with help.
4. Perform simple grooming—wash face, brush hair.
5. Help with bed making. Words can make a big difference in your child's attitude about his room. Do not say, "Run along now, I'll make the bed." Instead try, "I'll be happy to help you make your bed. I'll straighten the covers, and you can put your pillow on."
6. Tidy bedroom. Request your child's help with a happy, firm "Let's get with it" attitude. Praise him promptly.

Before Cartoons or Play

Empty bathroom wastebasket.

Before Lunch

1. Pick up toys and put in proper place.
2. Empty own hamper and take dirty clothes to washing area.

Monday Through Friday

1. Bring in newspaper and put in assigned place.
2. Keep pillows straightened on living room sofa.
3. Place magazines in a rack or basket.
4. Carry own dishes from the table and place on counter.
5. Empty small wastebaskets in bathroom or bedroom.
6. Use a child's mop or sponge to wipe up a small area.
7. Could use a child's broom or dustmop on uncarpeted floor.

Saturday–Family Team Time

1. Use a damp sponge to wipe off fingerprints from woodwork (sponge in small plastic bucket).
2. Join family with yard litter patrol (you may be surprised by how many leaves and papers can be collected in a little sand bucket).

Tips for Parents

1. When spills occur, let your child wipe up his own accidents.
2. Teach children to make simple choices: a half glass of orange juice or a full glass.
3. Remember the magic words, "Please" and "Thank you."

Chore Ideas for Children

4-5-year-olds

New skills should be matched with increased challenges. Try *four* chores a day!

Suggested Chores

Daily Before Breakfast

1. Dress.
2. Hang pajamas on hook.
3. Perform simple grooming—wash face, brush hair, brush teeth.
4. Help with bed making.
5. Tidy bedroom with help.

Before Cartoons or Play

1. Help clear breakfast table and load dishwasher.
2. Take old newspapers to trash.

Before Lunch

See chores for three-year-olds.

4:00 Pick-up

1. Put inside and outside playthings away.
2. Set table for dinner.

Before Story and Bedtime

1. Straighten room (with help).
2. Prepare for bed.
3. Take dirty clothes to washing area.

Monday Through Friday

1. Set the table.
2. Get the mail and put in proper place.
3. Sweep kitchen floor (child-size broom).
4. Dust bookcase or low shelves.
5. Water plants or garden.
6. Empty kitchen trash.
7. Give clean water to dog.
8. Pick up toys and put tricycle in assigned garage area at four o'clock.
9. Wash hands and come to the table when called.
10. Help clear dinner table and load dishwasher.

Saturday–Family Team Time

1. Help make a simple dessert (Jello, instant pudding).
2. He loves to dig in yard. Assign a small yard area to be weed free, but stay close by.
3. Help put groceries away.
4. Wash off outside toys and equipment.

Tips for Parents

1. Attention span for chores is four minutes (more if water is involved).
2. He likes to help himself, bringing milk from the refrigerator and preparing cold cereal. He wants to make his own sandwiches and put food on his dinner plate.
3. Encourage a quiet time after lunch.
4. Do not spare the praise. It is better to have tried and failed than never to have tried at all.

Chore Ideas for Children
6-7-year-olds

A family that works together makes time to play together. Now it is *five* chores a day.

Suggested Chores

Daily Before Breakfast
1. Dress.
2. Hang pajamas on hook.
3. Perform simple grooming—wash face, brush hair, brush teeth.
4. Make bed.
5. Tidy bedroom.

Before School
1. Shake area rugs.
2. Feed fish.

After School
1. Hang up school clothes and change into play clothes (no after-school snacks until this is completed).

4:00 Pick-up
1. Help parent put away items that are out of place.
2. Give water to the dog.

Before Dinner
Scrub potatoes for baking.

After Dinner
Wash dishes.

Before Story and Bedtime
1. Straighten room.
2. Place items for school by front door.

Monday Through Friday
1. Make bed (daily). Strip sheets on Monday and put in washing area.
2. Empty kitchen trash.
3. Bring in firewood.
4. Switch off unused lights.
5. Sweep outside—patio, porch, sidewalk, garage.
6. Wash bathroom sink.
7. Care for pets and living area.
8. Help prepare meals—make salad, scrub potatoes for baking.

Saturday–Family Team Time
1. Straighten books and game shelf.
2. Help arrange family bulletin board.
3. Rake leaves.
4. Water plants and flowers.
5. Wash plastic wastebaskets.
6. Wipe light switches.
7. Help put groceries away.

3. Prepare for bed.
4. Take dirty clothes to washing area.

Tips for Parents

1. Offer your child a choice of jobs. "No job" is no choice.
2. Always compliment your child for a job finished and well done.

Chore Ideas for Children

8-10-year-olds

Five chores a day with lots of time left to play.

Suggested Chores

Daily Before Breakfast

1. Dress.
2. Hang up pajamas or fold and place under pillow.
3. Perform simple grooming.
4. Make bed.
5. Help younger child make bed.
6. Tidy bedroom.

Before School

1. Practice music (twenty minutes).
2. Dust living room furniture.
3. Feed pets.

After School

1. Hang up school clothes and change to play clothes.
2. Clean up and ride bike to dentist or club meeting.

4:00 Pick-up

1. Empty all wastebaskets.

Monday Through Friday

1. Clean one cabinet or drawer in kitchen.
2. Clean own closet.
3. Feed the baby before family dinner hour.
4. Wash sink, toilet, and bathtub.
5. Clean up after pets in yard.
6. Pick fruit from trees.
7. Practice music (twenty minutes).
8. Scrape and stack dishes.
9. Wash or dry dishes.
10. Prepare a simple meal.
11. Strip bed weekly and wash sheets—can measure soap and use washer and dryer.
12. Sort wash by color, wash and dry, fold, and put away.

Saturday–Family Team Time

1. Do family mending (sew buttons, etc.)—hand work only.

2. Put away bike and play equipment.
3. Sweep patio and wash off patio table.

Before Dinner

1. Set table.
2. Set clocks (if needed).

After Dinner

1. Bring wood in (winter); pick fruit from trees (summer).
2. Clear table and do dinner dishes.

Before Story and Bedtime

1. Straighten room.
2. Do homework.
3. Place items for school by front door.
4. Prepare for bed.

2. Wash windows, mirrors.
3. Help adult clean out refrigerator (wipe off items as they are removed, then replace).
4. Wash combs and brushes.
5. Help clean linen closet—fold towels, tablecloths, and blankets neatly.
6. Polish toaster, coffee pot, or silverware.
7. Mop the floor.
8. Paint garage shelves.
9. Read simple recipe and cook (cleaning up is part of cooking).

Chore Ideas for Children

11-12-year-olds

Helping others should be encouraged, but remember, *your family* comes first with *five* chores a day.

Suggested Chores

Daily Before Breakfast

1. Dress.
2. Hang up pajamas or fold and place under pillow.
3. Perform simple grooming.
4. Make bed.
5. Help younger child make his bed.

Monday Through Friday

1. Make breakfast.
2. Pack lunches for family.
3. Help prepare dinner—scrub and bake potatoes, make salad.
4. Help serve dinner.
5. Load dishwasher or wash dishes.

6. Tidy bedroom.

Before School

1. Practice music (twenty minutes).
2. Vacuum traffic areas.

After School

1. Hang up school clothes and change into play clothes.
2. Take city bus to town—shop for hobby supplies.

4:00 Pick-up

1. Put bike in garage.
2. Rake leaves.

Before Dinner

Give baby its bottle.

After Dinner

1. Sweep kitchen floor.
2. Take out trash.

Before Bedtime

1. Put away hobbies.
2. Straighten room.
3. Do homework.
4. Put items for school by front door.
5. Prepare for bed, put clothes away.

6. Care for pets and living area.
7. Practice music (twenty minutes).
8. Vacuum traffic areas (before school).
9. Be banker (give milk money to children before school).

Saturday–Family Team Work

1. Wipe washer and dryer. Clean lint trap and washer filter.
2. Do the family wash.
3. Wipe off freezer.
4. Oil or wax furniture.
5. Help straighten garage.
6. Wash and oil bicycles.
7. Vacuum baseboards in entire house.
8. Make dessert for dinner.
9. Help Dad repair items outside.

As children grow older they become more and more involved in activities outside the home. Nevertheless, even a busy teenager should keep his own room clean, his clothes in order, and give some time to help the family. If you can run your home in an organized manner, you can keep his chore time to a minimum and still help him learn the self-discipline he must have.

"Students come into my office looking for a place to plug in their umbilical cords," said one college professor. "Parents fail to teach their children how to get along in this world, and they have to learn self-discipline when they leave home."

The time for systematic training is before your children leave home. Is there a skill your child needs that he has not yet learned?

To maintain systematic, day-to-day training through chores, you need to inject creativity and variety. When the family begins to tire of chore charts, shelve them for a few months and try something different. *Job jars* are a nice change. They appeal to everyone because of the element of surprise involved.

Cut twenty to thirty strips of paper and print on each one a job that needs to be done. Give the children a chance to offer suggestions for jobs, too. Drop the strips into the job jar. Children will rush to the jar each morning, eager to find out their jobs for the day. Parents should participate, too. It would not hurt for you to show some excitement about it. It can be a lot of fun and a pleasant way to get the work done. The following are job jar ideas:

- Wipe off every light switch plate.
- Clean the interior of the truck.
- Clean the leaves out of the ivy.
- Clean one kitchen drawer (ask Mom).
- Wash off washer and dryer (clean lint trap and washer lint filter).
- Pick up any paper or trash in front and back yards.
- Wipe off outside of freezer.
- Wash dog's bowls—sweep the area.
- Wipe off vacuum cleaner and clean string and lint off roller.
- Free turn!
- Ask Dad about a clean-up or garage job (one job).
- Clean interior of the car.
- Spot-check woodwork and wash off handprints.

Chore chart ideas are many and varied. To use the Saturday Round Robin Cards illustrated on page 119, simply list chores on three-by-five-inch cards. Prepare a chart having pockets, each labeled with the name of a family member. Rotate the cards from week to week.

The Lidens use a similar idea with their chore chart. They use

Brad	M	T	W	Th	F
1					
2					
3					
4					
5					
6					

Sue	M	T	W	Th	F
1					
2					
3					
4					
5					
6					

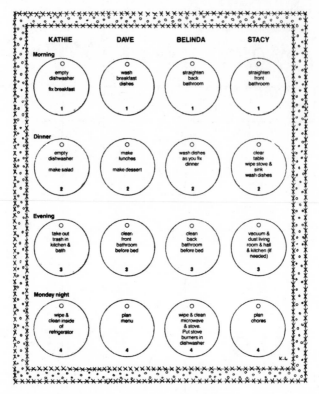

round disks with holes in the top and rotate the disks on Monday morning. Each turns his disk over when he finishes his chores. The back side of the disk is bright yellow.

The chart on page 117 lists chores and provides spaces for marking them off. This, too, can be done in a variety of ways. Use your imagination to produce your unique chart.

As you design your own chore chart, explain exactly what each job entails. Discuss the details of each assignment. If none of the charts illustrated here suits you, you can easily think of another type. Jobs listed here are for the purpose of illustration and may be quite different from those your family will do.

Remember, to succeed in assigning chores you must include your children in planning. Not only will they cooperate more willingly, but you will find yourselves giving more attention to

Card 1

Clean own bedroom
1. Put clean linens on bed
2. Spot-clean walls and woodwork
3. Clean mirror
4. Clean windows (if needed)
5. Dust
6. Empty wastebasket

Bathrooms (both)
1. As you enter, spray with cleaner on toilet, bathtub, and sink (while cleaner is working, wipe mirror and accessories)
2. Spot-clean walls and woodwork
3. Clean windows (if needed)
4. Scrub fixtures
5. Replace towels
6. Empty wastebasket
7. Wipe up floor

Card 2

Laundry
1. Wash and dry bedding and towels, put away
2. Wash bath mats and toilet covers (replace when dry)

Kitchen
1. Straighten one drawer of cabinet (worst one)
2. Clean inside of refrigerator
3. Wipe off table and chairs
4. Spray cleaner on sink, counter tops, and appliances. Cleaner can work while you spot-clean cabinet doors, walls, and woodwork. Scrub rest of sprayed areas
5. Empty trash
6. Shake area rugs
7. Sweep floor and mop

Card 3

Clean own bedroom
1. Put clean linens on bed
2. Spot-clean walls and woodwork
3. Clean mirror
4. Clean windows (if needed)
5. Dust
6. Empty wastebasket

Living room, entry, and hall
1. Vacuum and mop entryway
2. Water houseplants (entire house)
3. Spot-clean walls and woodwork
4. Clean windows (if needed)
5. Dust
6. Vacuum upholstery
7. Straighten magazines in rack; throw out old newspapers
8. Vacuum baseboards (carpeted area except family room)
9. Vacuum carpets in living room, hall, and bedrooms

Card 4

Clean own bedroom
1. Put clean linens on bed
2. Spot-clean walls and woodwork
3. Clean mirror
4. Clean windows (if needed)
5. Dust
6. Empty wastebasket

Family room
1. Straighten bookcase and magazines
2. Sweep fireplace hearth
3. Wipe off fireplace tools (use damp paper towels)
4. Spot-clean walls and woodwork
5. Dust
6. Clean TV screen and sliding glass door
7. Vacuum upholstery
8. Vacuum baseboards and carpets

suiting the work to the child's ability. If you work with them, you will find your house will run amazingly well and everyone will profit. This is one time you can have your cake and eat it, too.

GIVE YOUR CHILD CONFIDENCE

Do things for your children, and they will get along today; but teach them how to do things for themselves, and they will get along for the rest of their lives. Teaching your children to help themselves is basic to healthy self-esteem and the ability to function cooperatively in a marriage themselves when they grow up.

While a child lives under the protection and support of his parents, that child, whether male or female, should learn every skill he needs to be independent. A few are: care for his own clothes—clean, mend, sew on buttons; plan, shop for, cook, and serve a meal; bake bread, pastries, and cookies; clean the house; strip and change beds; mow, prune, and weed; change car oil, change a tire, and know the basics about how a car works; paint, wallpaper, and saw a board; do financial planning, budgeting, and shopping for all his own needs.

Eighteen years go by quickly. When a youngster reaches that magic number, he becomes an adult. If he has been taught everything he needs to know to live independently, he will go into the world with confidence.

The greatest gift you can give your child is a feeling of self-confidence and self-worth. If he feels confident and of worth, he will make a good marriage partner, a good parent, and a productive Christian.

Why do we ignore our children until they do something annoying? Instead, look for every opportunity to reinforce positive behavior. Catch them when they are pleasing you, and tell them how much you appreciate what they do. Never spare the praise.

Set rules in positive statements. "Walk in the house" instead of "Don't run in the house." "Let's talk in soft voices" instead of "Don't yell." If you want your children to speak quietly, then you must speak quietly.

Teach your children to look for the good in each other, too. The following are some of the things we do in our family to build self-image.

Once a year we take turns celebrating family members. The first week we celebrate Father. On family night he chooses the dinner and the family activity. We all try to be extra kind to him on his special day. It is like having a birthday without having to add a year.

The next week we celebrate Mother, then Janeé, then Eric, and finally Carla. One year we made posters announcing who was being celebrated and listing eight to ten qualities we admired in that person. Another year we chose a symbol for our honoree. A tall stout tree, for example, symbolized Everett, because he is our strength, and he points us to God (the children's idea).

One family night we made paper dolls representing each family member. On each doll were the words "——— is loveable and capable."

Then we wrote on every doll something we liked about that person. We pinned the dolls on the family bulletin board. When someone felt the need for a little infusion of confidence, he could read all the nice things his family had written about him on his doll.

Another night we made awards for each member of the family. After finishing these, we had a presentation ceremony. It was fun to decide what significant achievement each one had made. Our family peacemaker, for example, had her name printed on a dove, which was awarded to her.

Trophies, posters, and paper dolls are finally put on bulletin boards in the children's rooms. There is no way to measure the self-confidence they bring as a child looks at them day after day.

Once we drew names on family night. During the following week we kept track of the nice things the person whose name we had did. The next family night we read our list aloud.

A game we play on family night builds self-image, too. Put pictures of family members in envelopes. Take turns picking up an envelope. Everyone tries to guess whose picture you have by the clues you give. Clues are positive statements such as: "This person is very cheerful," or "He makes me feel good, because of the things he says," and so on.

Admiration, praise, and respect give the family the foundation on which to build lasting relationships and an atmosphere conducive to learning and growth.

GIVE THE CHILDREN A FEELING OF BELONGING

Your family is unique, and each one contributes to its specialness. Teamwork is the key to everything you do as a family. Work together. Seek the same goals. Support each other. It is this kind of teamwork you want to achieve.

The children must have a voice in family rules, how the chores will be done, and what the family will do. If the child feels like a member of the partnership, he will cooperate in the family system. He will become a willing learner, sharing responsibility, and growing "in keeping with his individual gift or bent."

To raise responsible children, then, start early to build good habits, teach by example, make work easy and varied, give your children confidence, and foster a feeling of belonging.

We have not talked about homework. Actually, the responsibility for homework is between your child and his teachers. Parents should know what is going on, and they should provide a quiet place for children to study. This may mean no television on school nights, or it may mean restrictions for children who do not allow enough time for homework.

Do not be drawn into doing the child's homework for him. Children learn very early how to make this happen. If you find yourself worrying about your youngster's term project or his daily homework, you are probably too involved. It is his problem, not yours, so let him do his own worrying. He has to learn to handle his own responsibilities before he can become a responsible person.

7

Money Is a Family Affair

MONEY IS IMPORTANT

A friend confided that she and her husband had gone bankrupt. "It's miserable," she said, sobbing. "I don't know how we got into such a terrible mess! I know one thing for sure—I'm going to teach my kids how to handle money so they never have to face the shame we are feeling right now!"

About 247,000 Americans filed for bankruptcy last year. Researchers have dug deep into family problems to try to find out what happened. The same money problems kept surfacing:

1. Poor training, especially in the teen years
2. No understanding of importance of keeping simple records
3. Poor communication and "team spirit" between couples
4. Being credit card "junkies"
5. No emergency fund
6. Overhousing: forty-five to fifty percent of income going for a roof over their heads and upkeep
7. Food taking up to thirty-five percent of income because of lack of basic cooking and shopping skills

123

8. Biggest problem: Have not learned the important words *"No, we can't afford it!"*

Disagreement over money heads the list of troublemakers in marriage. Most experts estimate that at least seventy-five percent of all divorces can be traced to clashes over finances. Whatever the percentage, the cold, hard fact remains—financing a marriage requires considerable attention and skill.

It also requires getting priorities straight. Jesus told us, "No one can serve two masters; for either he will hate the one and love the other, or he will hold to one and despise the other. You cannot serve God and mammon [money]" (Matthew 6:24).

Then He sets down the highest priority. "But seek first His kingdom and His righteousness; and all these things shall be added to you" (Matthew 6:33).

We hear such slogans as "Buy now, pay later," "Instant credit," "No money down," "Use your charge," "Easy payments." Could it be that the world of advertising and materialism in which we live has made us deaf to God's call to put Him first? Could it be that the sin of covetousness has taken over our lives?

Tom and Marjorie, a fine young Christian couple, have been married seven years, but their marriage is in trouble.

"It just seemed to creep up on us," says Marjorie bitterly. "Five dollars a month seemed so easy. Then all of a sudden there were so many bills coming in each month that we just couldn't meet the payments. We even went to a local finance company. They charged thirty-six percent interest just to lump small bills into one easy payment. But they turned us down!"

"This is an embarrassing situation," says Tom. "We don't want to file for bankruptcy. We just want a little help with lowering our monthly payments so we can pay our bills."

Tom and Marjorie got help in a Consumer Credit Counseling office. There are more than two hundred of these offices throughout the United States. They usually charge two to ten dollars per month to handle your creditors. They help you decide how much you can realistically set aside to pay debts each month, and then they get in touch with each one of your creditors to work out a payment plan. You may have to surrender your credit cards to your counselor until your debts are paid. To get the address of the office closest to you, write: National Foundation for Consumer Credit, 1819 H Street, Suite 510, Washington, D.C. 20006.

Consumer counselors work with people of all income levels. In one office a doctor sought help for his money problems. His collection of unpaid bills totaled $200,000. Another man had become a credit card "junkie." His counselor loaned him a pair of scissors to cut up fifty-three credit cards. The same office was counseling three certified public accountants. If such trained professionals have trouble managing money, we should not feel so bad when "ordinary folks" like us sometimes become overwhelmed by money matters.

Background, education, attitudes, and conditioning have everything to do with spending and money management patterns. The following illustrates what can happen when couples with conflicting money management patterns marry.

Mike and Jane came to marriage with the usual differences in background. They met, fell in love, and declared they were going to have one of the best marriages ever.

In time they had four children. Now they have been married fifteen years, and their marriage has deteriorated, leaving them bewildered and angry. They still love each other, but each has built up resentment against the other. What went wrong?

Mike spends many hours working, and he is very successful. He measures success by the amount of money he can make. He thought that being a good provider made him a good husband. He did love his family very much and was working hard to provide a comfortable home and living.

It seemed natural for Mike to handle the money, because he liked bookwork. He and Jane never talked about goals or priorities in their marriage. They made no family budget or joint long-range plan. Mike exclusively controlled the money. Jane refers to their money as "his money."

Mike gives Jane an allowance for groceries. He tells her to use charge accounts for whatever she and the children need. The receipts are good records of her spending.

Jane hates to run out of grocery money, because when she goes to Mike she feels like she is "begging" or is a "poor manager" of what funds she does have. She has no guidelines for spending with the charge accounts. She does not even know how much money is coming in.

One time she spent several days looking for just the right color in bathroom rugs and bought them for a good price. Mike happened to be paying bills that night and considered the charge accounts too high. To prevent an argument, Jane quietly returned the rugs.

At times Mike lavishes expensive gifts on Jane and the children. A few days after the bathroom rugs incident, he spent a large sum of money for luxurious accomodations in a resort area for a weekend and then wondered why all this luxury failed to impress Jane.

All Jane could think about that weekend was the thirty-dollar one-way fight they had had. "I'll be in the poorhouse if you don't stop buying all these things! Don't you know how hard I work and break my back for every dollar I make?"

Jane remembered thinking at the time, *Don't you know how many hours I shopped for those rugs, and how I have to make every dollar of my household money count?* She had said nothing aloud.

Many people are like Mike and Jane. They do not fight over money. They just do not discuss it. When husbands and wives avoid the discussion of money problems and objectives because they are afraid such talk will lead to more serious disagreements and quarrels, they are merely compounding the problem instead of facing it. Avoiding money discussions leads to avoidance of other communication, and "gunnysacking" feelings over a period of time can lead to crisis blowups and sometimes divorce.

Money ranks high among male goals. Many men, like Mike, evaluate their success on the basis of how much money they can make. Women, too, often control the money and the family.

Money is simply a medium of exchange, but it gets tangled up in emotional complexities—love, power, family relationships, self-worth. People feel a sense of power when they control with money.

Men who control the family's income while doling out a household allowance—and women who assume that if they work their earnings belong to them to spend on themselves—seem to believe that selfishness is normal. The common good and the interests of the family must take precedence over selfish individual interests.

That does not mean that a woman's earnings may not be used on the frills that make living more pleasant, but that decision should be made jointly. For a marital partnership to succeed, both husband and wife should share in financial decision making. All money earned, whether by him or by her, goes into one pot. From there it may be put into funds that may be handled by one or the other.

Before you can do a good job of allocating money, you need to know something about your needs and wants. We live in a time when our wants have been translated into needs. We no longer think of a television set, for example, as an extreme luxury.

If we only had to supply our needs—food, shelter, clothing, and transportation, we would have no problem. Deciding which of our strong desires are most important can lead to misunderstanding and disagreement. We must take time to find out what each member of the partnership considers important.

SPEND AN IMAGINARY MILLION

What could be more fun than to spend $1 million? And that is exactly what you should do! If you are a couple contemplating marriage, a childless couple, or a couple with children, imagine that a million-dollar windfall has come to you, and each of you will spend it just as you please.

Talking about how you would spend $1 million should stimulate interest in what you would do with money if you had it and perhaps in some impractical dreaming as well. It should also get you started thinking about long-range goals.

After you have had plenty of time for discussion, narrow the amount of the windfall to $50,000. Pass out paper and pencils this time. Then seek out spots where each of you can be alone to spend the $50,000 on paper. After you have made a list of the things you would buy, check the items most important to you. Give them a number rating: one, two, three, and so on.

At this point introduce your family to your family money book, a standard three-ring notebook that you should purchase before you begin your game of spending. How about a bright green book to symbolize $$$$$! This book will become an essential part of family business.

Get together again and compare your lists. Take a clean sheet of paper from your green money book. Divide it into two or three columns, depending on whether your children are old enough to participate. Label the columns his, hers, and theirs. In each column list in order of importance how each member of the family would spend the $50,000.

Now you will have some basis for deciding questions of value. Are two cars necessary for your family? Should you spend money for insulation? Air conditioning? Which appliances are most important? Can you get along without a clothes dryer? A washing machine? A dishwasher? Will you want to spend money for travel?

It would be a good idea to discuss what percentage of the family income you plan to return to God. A recognition that "everything I have or am comes from God" may lead to a commitment that will bring a warm feeling of satisfaction and accomplishment. Returning a fair share of God's bounty, many tithers find, not only takes faith but strengthens faith.

If you have never tithed before, you may want to start by giving four, five, or six percent of your income and set a goal of full tithing at some future date. Then joyously give to God before you spend for anything else. This will set the tone for keeping your priorities straight.

> Honor the LORD from your wealth,
> And from the first of all your produce
> (Proverbs 3:9).

Spend some time talking about what you want to get out of life and your hopes for the future. What are your lifetime goals? Where do you want to be financially at various stages of your life? Accept the fact that no income you ever earn will be enough to satisfy all your wants. Unfortunately, it is difficult for most of us to follow Paul's advice to be content with what we have. The more we earn the more we want.

Take plenty of time to talk. You may even want to continue the discussion for several days. Businessmen spend weeks setting up their goals, plans, and ideas. When you are ready, sit down as a couple or family and make up a family list.

Your master plan should take into account all financial needs and wants—benevolence, insurance, housing, emergency fund, savings, education, special trips, car. Include priority items that appeared on individual lists.

Finally, take this family list and go through it, numbering each item in order of importance. From your basic financial goals you must determine your money objectives and target dates for reaching them.

Financial Goals

Goal	$Cost	Date Begun	Achievement Date

Or, list two items you would like to have, one within the next month, the next within a year. Divide the "year" item into twelve and set aside that amount each month.

Or, use this concept:

Things I need and want in the next three months	Cost	Things I want after three months	Cost
1.	1.	1.	1.
2.	2.	2.	2.

If you can make it through this process with no casualties, you will be in good shape to set up your money plan.

YOUR MONEY PLAN—A JOINT PROJECT

Looking at the list of things you need and want is probably discouraging when you think of the little money you have. Perhaps you think if you actually had $1 million to spend you would have no problems. Most of us think everything would be all right if we had more money. Not so! As hard as it is to believe, the size of your income is not nearly as important as what you do with it.

Many people earn on one income level and spend on another. When this happens, there will be pressures. Money dominates such families, because there is never enough of it.

Fred, a dentist who practices in a large California city, has experienced this. He and his wife, Susan, did without many things while he finished his schooling. Immediately after he went to work, they began buying the things they had wanted for so long.

Fred's practice grew, and so did his spending. He bought a luxurious $150,000 home with its own tennis court. Fred and Susan's two children attended a private school. The family rode in a brand-new station wagon, and Fred had a Scout to take on hunting trips. New clothes spilled out of two large walk-in closets.

Even with the large income Fred earned from his dental practice, he could not afford so much luxury. Harsh words, unhappiness, and a gnawing sense of uneasiness and worry became common in their home.

Fortunately, Fred and Susan gradually had their eyes opened to what had gone wrong. They sold the home they dearly loved, bought a $40,000 tract house, and now live within their means. Contentment and peace have replaced the storminess they once knew. Few couples who live above their income are lucky enough to remedy their situation before bankruptcy hits or the marriage dissolves.

To learn how to manage money and to understand something about buying power, start with the nickles and dimes and dollars. If you cannot manage a small income, you probably would be unable to manage a large one.

No one would think of starting a business partnership without carefully organizing the finances needed to support that business. Neither would one partner take on the total responsibility for planning how that partnership should be financed without letting the other partners know what was going on. Financing a marital partnership must be just as carefully organized and planned by all the partners.

Involving your family in the business of running the home has many benefits.

First, if everyone (husband, wife, and older children) has a part in planning, most of the potential for squabbles and dissatisfaction will be eliminated. You will have far greater cooperation in reaching the goals set by all of you. Arbitrary decisions invite resentment.

Second, involving your children in the financial planning of the family gives them a once-in-a-lifetime apprenticeship and an invaluable opportunity to become good managers, too.

Third, you will have access to more than one mind. You can bounce your ideas off others who care as much as you do about the success of the operation. Even if you are a financial genius, getting outside opinions will still be to your advantage.

Just a word of caution. If you are already head over heels in debt and are genuinely worried about the family finances, do not bring your children into this situation. They need to understand something about the family financial limitations, but they do not need to carry the burden of the worry.

Your family unit—large or small—is an organization with income, outgo, and an accumulation of assets. The better you keep records on this organization, the more effectively it functions.

It takes no magic to become organized financially. First, turn a selected place in the house into a money mangement center. Keep this area as free from clutter as you can. Can you imagine a bank manager's desk piled high with torn-out recipes, new fishing hooks, unanswered letters, schoolbooks, birthday cards and invitations, coats, sweaters, and undeveloped film?

If you are setting up a family money plan, make sure your surroundings do not work against you. A small investment in equipment can save money, time, and frustration later. If you can obtain a desk or practical writing surface, place it where you can work without distraction.

In your management center keep all the family records. Set up envelopes or files to hold receipts and canceled checks by categories. Your green family money book belongs here, too. Just knowing where you can find things takes much of the drudgery out of record keeping.

Items you will need to equip the center include: calendar, pencils and pens, paper clips, paper and envelopes, postage stamps, wastebasket, Scotch tape, scissors, ruler, rubber bands, postcards, small memorandum pad, stapler, telephone book, address book, good lighting, files, brown envelopes, green money book, stationery, and checkbook.

Once your management center is set up, you can begin the simple steps necessary to achieve financial control. Like running any business, you must periodically look at your assets, set financial goals, and then come up with a plan that will help you meet those goals. A plan gives you time. And it should prevent that basic threat to sound money management, impulsiveness in buying and borrowing.

Many standard business practices work well in family finances. We have already talked about mapping a plan to achieve specific objectives within a stated period. We did this by playing the "spending an imaginary million" game. The financial goals you set up from this activity became page one in your green family money book. Businessmen call this "management by objectives."

Simple, isn't it? The next step is a standard business practice called "cash flow accounting." That is a long name for a simple process that involves matching the amount of money coming in from all sources to the amount going out for all purposes.

The first thing you must do is find out how much money you have coming in. Write down every item of income you expect during the year. Estimate each item of income as accurately as you can. When in doubt, put down the minimum. List only net amounts. Convert each total to a monthly figure.

Next, list all of your family's fixed expenses—church, mortgage payments or rent, utilities, insurance, car payment, installment loans, car expense, tuition, and so on. Any money left after fixed expenses are paid is called discretionary income. The more you have, the easier it will be to manage.

The good manager divides the big items into monthly payments so that the money will always be there when the yearly payment comes due. A $360 annual insurance payment will never panic you if you put aside $30 a month to prepare for it. Failure to do so could cause a serious financial crisis.

Now take another clean sheet of paper from your green money book and set up a statement something like this. Totals are monthly figures.

Fixed payments	Payment		Payment
House payment	_____	Taxes	_____
Group 1: Installments	Payment	Months left to pay	Balance
_____	_____	_____	_____
_____	_____	_____	_____
_____	_____	_____	_____
_____	_____	_____	_____
Total	_____	Total	_____
Group 2: Utilities		Group 3:	Payment
Phone	_____	Car gas	_____
Electricity	_____	Car insurance	_____
Water	_____	Other insurance	_____
Gas	_____	Church/donations	_____
Others	_____	Club dues	_____
Total	_____	Newspaper	_____
		Magazines	_____
		Total	_____

Group 4: Unpaid bills		Total Expenses	
_____	_____	House	_____
_____	_____	Taxes	_____
_____	_____	Group 1	_____
Total	_____	Group 2	_____
		Group 3	_____
Monthly take-home pay	_____	Total	_____
Monthly outgo	_____		
Left to live on	_____		

There are 4⅓ weeks in a month. This means we have $_____ per week to spend. This amount must cover clothes, doctor bills, savings, et cetera.

Assets	Liabilities
Checking account _____	Bills _____
Savings account _____	
Cash on hand _____	
Total _____	Total _____

Your plan should include a certain amount of money set aside for emergencies. You may want to reach for $300 as a beginning, but later try for $1,000. Many people find this a practical sum. Some people call this a slush fund. Unexpected bills, such as for car repair, patching a leaky roof, or fixing a fence blown down by the wind, are often the last strand that breaks the rope unless you are ready for them. Whenever you withdraw money from this emergency fund, you should pay it back as quickly as possible to insure a constantly available emergency cushion.

Some people find it helpful to keep a spending record for a short period of time. Such a record can help you find hidden leaks in your spending. One way to do this is to attach a sheet of paper to the refrigerator or kitchen bulletin board. Every night each person records every purchase made during the day, including dimes for parking meters and quarters for coffee or Cokes. In a few weeks you will be able to see where your money is going.

You can use this record or checkbook records to help you set up your money plan (cash flow accounting). One couple worked out a plan that was so successful that many families with limited income have used their method.

Their form looked something like this:

Date _____ to _____ 19___

Income

	Bills	Owe	Pay	Left to pay
Tim _____				
_____				
Shawn _____				
_____				
Total _____ Total				

Budget

	Planned	Spent	Saved	Total extra
House				
Food				
Church				
Car				
Gas (car)				
Clothes				
Household				
Medical				
Insurance				
Electricity				
Water				
Garbage				
Telephone				
Gas				
Misc.				
Total				

Income _____   Savings _____ Slush fund _____
Budget _____   Prior savings _____ Prior slush _____
Bills _____   Total savings _____ Total slush _____
Savings _____
or Slush Fund _____

Use the amount in the total-extra column to pay off bills faster and to build a savings account. By using this budget, the couple who put it together were able to start a savings account for the first time since they had been married. They still use this form, and praise the Lord for it. You might, too!

Knowing what your income will be over a certain period of time and how much of it can be used for any purchase gives you a basis for wise use of credit. Businesses have special methods for determining how much they can borrow. A rule of thumb for the home is never let debt (excluding mortgage) get higher than twenty percent of your annual net income. Only you can decide when going into debt makes good financial sense. It takes a great deal of skill to use debt as an effective money management tool to achieve goals, so do not use it unless you are sure you have those skills.

Businesses keep an up-to-date record of their net worth, and you should too. To do this, draw up a balance sheet of all your assets and liabilities. On one side of a sheet of paper list your assets and what they are worth. This list will include house, car, camera equipment, bank accounts, art collection, stocks and bonds, and so on. On the other side list your liabilities—mortgage, debts, et cetera.

This list will give you some idea of what you are worth. If your assets are greater than your liabilities, you are in good shape. If your liabilities are greater than your assets, you have a big problem!

Once all this information is in hand, setting up a workable family money plan will be incredibly easy. When everyday money problems become serious and when serious problems become critical, your green money book will show you at a glance where you stand financially and what you need to do about it. Control will always be at your fingertips.

EVERYONE NEEDS AN ALLOWANCE

Husbands and wives should be allotted a small amount of money to spend as they choose. This money need not be accounted for. Children, too, should share in the family income. All children benefit from handling money themselves. Children's allowances do not fall into the category of "do your own thing" in the same way parents' allowances do. Their allowances are a learning tool, and they must learn to spend them first on needs and second on wants.

Children need fixed amounts given at specified times so they know where they stand. The amount must relate to the child's needs, the size of the family income, and to some extent to what other children his age have to spend.

It is very important that the entire allowance is not allocated by parents. Every child should have a discretionary income, too. If every penny must go for school lunches, church, specified savings, Scout dues, or piano lessons, the child will feel just as trapped as adults do when they have no money of their own to spend in their own way. Even more important, they will not learn much about money management.

On the other hand, children should not be given money and told they can do anything they like with it. Parents need to set guidelines. Children can spend their money on what they want within the framework of the family standards.

For example, if you have carefully controlled the amount of snacks and sweets your children eat, you should not disregard those standards simply because the child wants to spend his "own" money. If, however, he has decided on a toy that you can see is cheaply made, you may want to point out its drawbacks, but let him decide whether to buy it. If he pays fifty-six cents for a toy that breaks within half an hour after he gets it home, he will learn a valuable lesson that may save him much more than that when he is older.

A child learns from his mistakes. If he is satisfied with his purchase, it was a good choice no matter what you think. If he is not satisfied, he will not make that choice again.

Throughout the elementary school ages, the allowance should be given weekly. It is easiest for parents to remember a specified day, and a week is a manageable unit for the child. By the time youngsters reach high school, most of them can go on a monthly budget. By this time they should have experience at record keeping and have enough skill to buy many of their own needs including clothes.

How much the allowance should be can be a problem. Begin by giving a young child, three, four, or five years old, a quarter a week to spend on the things he wants. When the ice-cream man comes by, let him decide if he wants to spend his quarter on an ice-cream bar. He will soon learn that there is an end to the money available for things like that.

An allowance should also eliminate the endless running to Mother or Daddy to beg for money. When his money is gone, tell him firmly that is all there is until the next time his allowance is due.

When the child enters school, his needs increase. He must handle many of them himself. The kindergarten child, for example, takes his own milk money to school. Instead of doling out a dime a day, make this a part of his allowance. This will teach him how to make money last over a period of time. Your adding the milk money to the discretionary amount already in the allowance, will also teach him how to have something left over. Consequently, he learns the basic skills in money management, budgeting and saving.

The young child must develop his own spending standards. You can expect impulse buying at first. It takes time for him to learn that hanging on to money provides larger amounts to buy better things. Only by trial and error can he learn how to handle money wisely.

In deciding what to give elementary age children, consider the specific needs of each child. Take the time to find out what the things he wants to buy actually cost. Figure out what items his allowance must cover. Too little money makes the allowance meaningless. On the other hand, too much money makes children uneasy and is not a realistic learning tool.

Be flexible. Try an amount you have all agreed upon and see how it works out. This weekly or monthly stipend should be consistent and never influenced by other considerations. It should not be withheld for punishment or increased as a reward. Money should be free of emotion and as impersonal as possible.

If the child is always short, and he has made a reasonable effort to manage his money well, be willing to sit down and discuss it with him. What went wrong? Where is his money going? Perhaps he needs to consider a savings plan to reach his spending objectives. If you can see that he really needs more money, renegotiate the amount of the allowance. Remember, as your child grows, his needs grow also. Furthermore, he can handle more and more of his own spending. This means an increase in allowance, of course.

One mother allows her children to buy their own socks when they become old enough to read. As they grow older she increases the amount of their own clothing they buy. By the time they reach high school, they can shop intelligently for all of their clothes.

Many parents report that it is best to give a clothes allowance separate from the children's regular allowance By doing this, you remove the temptation to spend money given for clothes on other things. Some parents give their teenage children their clothes allowance quarterly or every two months.

"My boys take much better care of their clothes since they began buying them themselves," says one father. "When I bought their clothes they were very nonchalant about taking care of them. Now they get twenty dollars a month to buy clothes. They coast through summer going barefooted and wearing cutoffs. That gives them a chance to save for the heavy fall buying. They have more time to do comparative shopping, too. They know which store has the best buy on every item of clothing they need."

Some parents increase their children's allowances for a month or two at Christmastime, but perhaps one mother has a better plan. She helps her children save for Christmas by taking them to the bank right after Christmas to open a Christmas account. Each week a small portion of their allowances goes into their Christmas plan. The first time they got their twenty-five dollar Christmas Club check, they were overwhelmed by the amount of money they had to spend for Christmas gifts. It taught them a valuable lesson about the power of saving even small amounts.

Allowances, then, give adults the means to gratify personal whims without damaging the welfare of the family. For children, allowances serve a twofold purpose. It gives them money to manage for their needs and money to spend for their wants.

MONEY TEACHES RESPONSIBILITY

If you want your children to grow up to be responsible earners and consumers, you must teach them how to handle money. Arrayed against you in all their power are a multitude of giant corporations determined to get their share of your child's pocket money.

Kids' spending is big business. They have more than $50 billion a year in disposable income. "Children are the most easily swayed group of consumers in this country," says Melvin Helitzer, New York advertising man. "I am frightened at the power we as marketers have over forty million people who in turn influence their parents and others."[1]

Today's youth spend more than twenty percent of all their waking hours with mass media. Television accounts for by far the largest portion of this time. Parents must control their children's television habits. When they do watch, turn it into an advantage by using television commercials as a basis for consumer education. The materialistic and sometimes unhealthful demands generated by commercials can be denied. Do not let your young television viewer dictate what kind of cereals to buy.

Parents' attitudes and examples set the tone for a child's approach to money management. In fact, counselors claim this can be a problem when adults are unaware that their own attitudes toward money—how they feel about spending and saving, paying in cash or buying on credit, which spouse pays the bills—reflect the ways their parents dealt with finances. When partners come from different backgrounds, they need to resolve these questions about money on a mature level, or there will always be financial conflict.

If you as parents can handle your finances confidently and fairly successfully, your children will probably be able to handle their finances with little trouble. They reflect your attitudes about women working, who controls the family purse strings, the value of accumulating material possessions, the importance of having a car as luxurious as the neighbors, and much more.

You will not have much success teaching your children to be honest in their financial dealings if they hear you tell the cashier at the zoo that Junior is under twelve when he is actually thirteen. They will not patiently wait to save money for a bicycle if they see you buy what you want when you want it even if it means buying on credit. You have heard before, and it is true: children learn from what they see you do, not from what they hear you say.

They also learn from doing, and you can be an effective teacher. When you hand the child his allowance, help him work out a sensible spending plan for it. As soon as he understands figures, provide him with a cashbook, and teach him how to enter his balance and thereafter record his expenditures and income, adjusting the balance on hand.

You can also teach children something about spending on a short-term basis. For a seven-day period have them keep a reasonably accurate record of daily earnings and expenses.

Children are never too young to begin learning how to be good managers. Even a toddler can be taught the importance of turning off lights that are not being used, closing the bedroom doors to save on the heat, using only as much toilet paper as he actually needs.

If you take your children marketing with you, plan for extra time to teach them why you make the choices you do. Explain unit pricing to them, and show them how it works. Teach them to read labels and get the best buy for their money. Show them how to select ripe fruit. When you get home, let your children stack the canned goods in such a way that the family will eat first the

Personal Spending for Seven Days

Dates: From _____ Through _____

Income	Day 1	Day 2	Day 3	Day 4	Day 5	Day 6	Day 7	Total
Money received or earned								
Expenses								
Tithes								
Lunches								
Club dues								
Hobbies								
Savings								
Gifts								
Personal								
Recreation								
Miscellaneous								
Total expenses								

Total income _____
Total expanses _____
Balance at end of seven days _____

food stored longest. Let them empty the fruits and vegetables into refrigerator drawers to preserve their freshness.

Take your children when you shop for other things, too. Teach them the differences between wool, cotton, and Acrilan. Show them labels, and explain that if you do not want to iron a shirt you buy wash-and-wear rather than cotton. At a very young age children can learn the differences in quality in differently priced socks or underwear. Girls learn that ruffles on underwear makes them less comfortable than plain underwear.

By the time your children become nine or ten, they can be an enormous help when you go grocery shopping. Tear or cut your grocery list into as many parts as you have people shopping. Specify a place where everyone can meet when he has gathered the items on his list.

There are many opportunities to teach children how to manage money. At one time Dave had his own business. He and Kathie taught their sixteen-year-old daughter to be the bookkeeper for the business as well as for the family. All family sales receipts went into a shoebox. At the end of the week, Belinda recorded them in the family cashbook.

In another family as each child reached his junior year in high school, he took over the job of managing the family checkbook—opening the bills, writing the checks, mailing deposits, keeping the balance up to date, and balancing the checkbook with the bank statement. He brought the checks to his father or mother for their signatures and approval.

If your teenager gets a sizeable allowance to buy his own clothes and pay all his own expenses, you might want to encourage him to open a checking account. Any bank will be glad to start one for him. Teach him how to reconcile checkbook and bank statement. It should be entirely his to handle.

The more responsibility for money you give your children, the more capable they become as money managers. And all under your observation and with your expert advice!

A child who is old enough to handle money is old enough to have some other responsibilities as well, but do not make one dependent on the other. If an allowance is to be an effective learning tool, parents must not demand work or good behavior as the price for it. When children have not cleaned their rooms or have been careless with coats, sweaters, or lunch pails, it is difficult to hand over their allowances as usual with a smile.

These problems are best dealt with in some other way. If my children neglect to clean their rooms, I tell them if I have to clean them I am very expensive, because my time is extremely valuable. I charge them a sizeable cleaning fee, and they do not hire me too often!

Do not pay for jobs done around the house (taking out the garbage, cleaning their rooms, cleaning up after the dog, sweeping the sidewalk). Such jobs are part of family responsibility.

The exception to this rule are "extra" jobs or the kind of work you might hire someone else to do. If you normally have your lawn mowed by a professional, and your son or daughter wants to take over, then pay him or her the going wage, but demand good work. If you mow your own lawn, your child should do the job when asked, just as you have done it in the past.

If you do hire your children, keep it just as businesslike as possible. Remember, you are not asking them to help; you are offering a job. Explain the job, offer a realistic rate of pay, and then permit the child to accept or reject it. If you insist that he do the job anyway, the money is a bribe and it is not a legitimate job offer. In this case, you are loading money with emotion, which is something you want to avoid doing.

As soon as possible, children should be taught that they must work for anything they want that is out-of-the-ordinary. The surest road to independence is through work outside the home. Children exercise a great deal of creativity thinking up jobs to do to earn extra money.

Dozens of Ways to Make Money by Yvonne Horn is an excellent source for young teens looking for ideas to make money. And of course, there are always chores to do for neighbors, wood to cut, lawns to care for, rooms to paint, children to watch, and pets to feed when their owners are on vacation.

Such jobs instill valuable lessons about money management. They give children a sense of purpose plus a realistic idea of the relationship between the time and effort necessary to earn a dollar and what that dollar can buy. My daughter looked stunned when she realized the hiking boots she wanted would cost the entire thirty dollars she had earned working all week cleaning house for an invalid.

A child's job should be suited to his ability, of course, and should not interfere with school work and other responsibilities. In some cases teens earning substantial amounts can take on most of their own expenses, especially if family income is severely limited.

Some parents are concerned about teaching their children to save some of their money. Saving money may mean one thing to adults and another to youngsters. To young children, saving is totally meaningless. Those pennies clinking into the piggy bank please Dad and Mom, but Junior may care little because he realizes that pennies deposited in his pig disappear forever anyway.

Trying to teach a child to save before he can comprehend large sums and when he still has little concept of time is futile. The older the child gets, the more his sense of time increases. As a child matures, you can encourage him to begin saving only if he has an immediate and reachable goal—one he can see, understand, want, and expect to get. Real motivation must come from within the child.

A child's earliest savings plans are really spending plans, and after reaching his goal, he should be encouraged to spend what he has saved. Purpose is the key. If children do not want to save for something, and saving is forced, the emphasis is on accumulation of money for its own sake rather than for what it can do.

It is much better for children to learn to use money, to spend it wisely, psychiatrists claim, than to hoard and never spend. Do not brag to visitors and friends about your child's thriftiness and how much money he has managed to accumulate. If he is overly cautious or has gained status through his massive bank account, encourage him to spend his money rather than to hoard it endlessly. Sooner or later he will want something you cannot get him. That is the time to suggest that he spend some of his savings to get what he wants.

Never forget that money is a practical tool to be used in daily living. It is essential to every marital partnership. Learning to use it wisely can help insure a lasting partnership and help guarantee that your children will become good managers, too. Making it a family affair is an absolute must.

8

How to Stretch the Family Dollar

CREATE SELF-PROTECTION INSURANCE

Since money experts agree that financial success does not depend on how much you make, but on what you do with what you make, stretching the family dollar is the key to good management. Families who develop an attitude of thrift can do far more with the same amount of money than families who do not learn thriftiness.

No insurance on the market can protect you from yourself. If you allow greed, speed, gullibility, or ignorance to control your spending habits you will always be in financial trouble. Be on the lookout for such weaknesses in yourself. If you recognize them for what they are, you can probably stamp them out.

To achieve financial success, most of us need to change our attitudes. Remember, thriftiness is an attitude. Pennies, nickles, and dimes make dollars. Never dismiss the chance to save a dime with the careless comment, "What good is a dime?" If you could manage to save a dime every day, at the end of a year you would have an extra $36.50. Saving 25¢ a day could build a fund of $500 in five years.

If you learn to think in terms of nickles and dimes and quarters, you will probably save much more than ten cents every day, because the wise money manager saves that amount over and over by intelligent shopping, learning how to avoid money pitfalls, making do with what he has, acquiring solid values, and knowing how to use skills to his advantage.

Earlier we talked about Jesus' parable concerning stewardship. Whether it is time or money that God has entrusted to our care, He expects us to use it wisely. Keep an open mind, and never stop looking for more information and better ways to improve financing your marital partnership. That kind of stewardship creates self-protection insurance that cannot be bought for any price. It is an important part of the abundant life that any Christian can enjoy.

MAKE DO WITH WHAT YOU HAVE

The easiest and most obvious way to stretch a dollar is to hang on to it as long as you can. To do this, you must make do with what you have.

Some of you can do that easily, because you have many things. If you fall into that category, and still never seem to have enough money to get you to the next payday, look critically at your possessions. What do you have that you really do not need? Make a list of the things you can do without. Then have a garage sale or run an ad in the newspaper to turn those assets back into money.

Do not fritter away this money. Use it where it will do the most good and relieve some of the pressure. Pay off old debts. Put it into a slush fund to protect you in emergencies. Or put some into your checking account to give you a cushion.

Grandmother could teach us a lot about how to make do. By copying her housekeeping know-how we can save money, too. For example, to deodorize a room, Grandma boiled five or six whole cloves in a pint of water for twenty minutes. A box of matches, another standard, inexpensive deodorizer she used, works well in the bathroom. Light a match and let it burn for a few seconds before blowing it out. The sulphur dispels unpleasant odors.

Grandma did a top-notch job of cleaning without buying a dozen expensive cleaners, each touted as the best way to get a particular job done. She needed only two cleaners—soda and ammonia.

This is all you do. To clean painted woodwork, walls, tile, and glass surfaces, use 3 tablespoons of soda to a quart of warm water. For all floors except wood, use ammonia. It cuts grease and dirt, and you will not need to rinse afterward. For regular cleaning, use 3 tablespoons of ammonia to 1 gallon of water. If you have a wax buildup, use a heavy solution, 1½ cups of ammonia to 1 gallon of water. If possible, open the windows to air out the house when you do your cleaning.

To clean a grease spot on your carpeting, brush dry soda into the stain and let it set overnight. Next morning vacuum up the soda and the stain.

Save left over soap pieces, too small for use. Then make soap jelly by pouring boiling water over them in a jar. Use this jelly for delicate washables.

When you wash your hair, follow the washing with a lemon or vinegar rinse—two tablespoons of lemon juice in the final rinse water for blondes, two tablespoons of vinegar for brunettes.

You can probably find many other ways to make do, but a time will come when you need or want to buy something you do not have. If you have limited funds, ask yourself these ten questions before you buy anything:

- Do I really need it, or can I get along with what I have?
- Can I make it?
- How often will I use it?
- Will it serve well in the way I want to use it?
- Could I choose something else that would serve this and other purposes too?
- How much care does it require?
- How durable is it?
- Does it have good design and quality?

- How much storage space does it require?
- What good information can I get to help me decide?

If you give each purchase this kind of careful consideration, you will probably buy nothing you do not need or should not have.

Smart Shopping Makes More Cents

To stretch your inflated dollar you must learn to "shop smart." At one end of the shopping mall I found a dress ten dollars cheaper than the same dress at the other end of the mall. If I can save ten dollars on one item by smart shopping, I am twelve dollars ahead—because what I save is tax-free. Saving what you have already earned and paid taxes on is more profitable than working for more pay.

There are some rules and principles every smart shopper must know and follow. First, let us consider some of these general rules. Then we shall discuss specific areas of shopping such as how to buy clothes, medication, furniture, and cars.

Never expect to buy something for nothing.

A legitimate merchant cannot stay in business if his margin of profit is too low. So expect to pay a reasonable price. Harden yourself to the attractive-sounding telephone "giveaways." They are designed to trap gullible people. Always remember, nobody is going to give you something for nothing.

Nearly every couple has to be suckered into a sale by a clever door-to-door salesman before learning to resist such pressure. With us it was a vacuum cleaner we had no intention of buying and with the Lidens it was a sewing machine. To this day I can hardly think about that vacuum cleaner without feeling a hard lump of anger rise to my throat.

Whether it is a vacuum cleaner, a freezer plan, or a furnace-cleaning job, you can always do better by thoughtful, careful shopping for what you want. Beware of people selling magazines, books, utensils, roofing or siding, sewing machines, and services at your door or by telephone.

If you make a purchase anywhere other than in a regular retail store make sure you know exactly what you are paying for. Street bargains should be treated with extreme caution. Fraud and bunco schemes take on many forms and are usually quite well disguised to the unaware customer.

Some roofing-driveway recoaters, for example, tell unsuspecting homeowners that they have just finished a job around the corner and "have just enough material left for one more roof or driveway." The coating is usually cheap diluted material that ruins the driveway or roof to which it is applied.

Do not be a victim of other dishonest selling techniques. If you receive unordered merchandise through the mail, the law now says that you can keep these goods, use them, and you cannot be billed for them.

Another technique often used by advertisers is "bait and switch." Merchants advertise lower-than-usual prices, featuring their low-price merchandise. When you go to the store, they try to sell you higher priced or "better quality" items. Do not let merchants influence you to "trade up" to more expensive models than you need or can afford.

BE AN INFORMED SHOPPER.

Select commodities that will not go out of fashion in a short time. Read labels. Ask questions about the wear and performance of the things you buy. You may find a good buy on an item marked "irregular." Manufacturers work under intense lighting. The imperfections they spot might not be noticeable to anyone else.

Find out the exact meaning of a warranty, or guarantee. What is included? What is not included? Who is responsible for what? Who pays for parts? Who pays for labor? Where do you call or go for service? How long is the warranty good?

Know what qualities you require in products you plan to buy and how to recognize the qualities you need. Compare prices in advertising, newspapers, and magazines. Check *Consumer Reports* and the *Consumer Bulletin*—both are nonprofit consumer testing organizations.

You can save ten to thirty percent by comparative shopping in food and much more in other goods. High prices do not always guarantee high quality. Check various kinds of stores—discount, mail order, chains, department stores, the small retailer, and cooperative stores.

Other places smart shoppers may look for bargains are factory outlets, independent factory-outlet stores, buyers' clubs, factory-outlet shopping malls, catalog warehouse showrooms, clearance centers, closeout stores, and distribution-center outlets, and sometimes you can buy directly from the manufacturer.

There are also discount diner and entertainment clubs such as the VIP Pass Club, Dine-Out Club, National Dining Club, and Sports Unlimited. Membership in these clubs for a small fee gives you two passes to dinners, lodging, and events for the price of one.

An organization in Florida called S.O.S., Inc. publishes a directory every year that contains over four thousand sources of bargains around the country and in Canada. S.O.S. stands for Save on Shopping. You can find out about it by writing to: S.O.S., Box 10482, Dept. FC, Jacksonville, Fla. 32207.

If you buy at craft or art shows and fairs, for best prices go on the last day. Since craftsmen and artists would rather not take their wares back home, you may be able to negotiate a better price.

NEVER GO SHOPPING ANYWHERE WITHOUT A SHOPPING LIST.

For expensive items like suits, furniture, and a new car, make a spending plan.

YOU CAN TAKE ADVANTAGE OF THE SEASONAL SALES AND EASILY SAVE HUNDREDS OF DOLLARS.

Do not forget to buy by the same principle at the grocery store.

There are three major periods for storewide clearance sales: after Easter, after July 4th, and after Christmas. Other well-known sales are those run for George Washington's birthday, Columbus Day, Veterans Day, the summer white sales, and so on.

Do not minimize the importance of planning your spending to take advantage of the rhythmic pattern of buying and selling. It is created by the ebb and flow of quantities of goods in stores and the lows and highs of consumer demand. It is just as important to know when to buy as it is to know how and where.

The following is a shopping calendar to help you plan intelligently:

January

After-Christmas sales, furniture, winter clothes, men's coats and shirts, lingerie, shoes, furs, handbags, costume jewelry, white sales of sheets, pillowcases, towels, tablecloths, toiletries, quilts, toys, dishes, sports equipment, small appliances, water heaters, freezers, and refrigerators.

February

Furniture, rugs, mattresses, curtains, bedding, china, glassware, housewares, notions, toys, art supplies, radios and phonographs, air conditioners, used cars, car seat covers, stereo equipment, silverware.

March

Winter coats, infants' wear, spring clothing, shoes, laundry appliances, luggage, skates, ski equipment, storm windows.

April

After-Easter clothes clearances, men's and boys' suits, women's and children's coats, housecoats, women's hats, clothes dryers, ranges.

May

Blankets, white sales, TV sets, soaps, cleaning aids, women's underwear, housecoats, handbags, sportswear, tires.

June

TV sets, summer clothes and fabrics, dresses, piece goods, refrigerators, storm windows, furniture, building materials, lumber.

July

Summer clothes, shoes, bathing suits, men's hats, infants' wear, lingerie, men's shirts, sportswear, handbags, used cars, washing machines, home appliances, toiletries and colognes, air conditioners, fuel oil, radios, phonographs, freezers, rugs and carpet, stereo equipment, summer sports equipment.

August

Summer furniture, mattresses, rugs, curtains, bedding, home furnishings, housewares, lamps, white sales, coats, furs, men's clothing, tires, lawn mowers, sprinklers, yard tools, barbecue sets and tools, camping equipment, air conditioners, carriages, new cars, paints, school supplies, school clothes, bathing suits, fans.

September

New cars, bicycles, batteries and mufflers, children's clothing, China, dishes, furniture, gardening equipment, glassware, hardware, housewares, lamps, paints, piece goods, rugs and carpet, tools.

October

Fishing equipment, china, glassware, hosiery, housecoats, school clothes, school supplies, silverware, cars.

November

Used cars, car seat covers, children's clothing, women and children's coats, dresses, housecoats, piece goods, quilts, men's and women's shoes, men's and boy's suits, ranges, water heaters.

December

Used cars, children's clothing, women's and children's coats, men's clothing, men's and women's shoes, party items, quilts. The day after Christmas is Bargain Day all over town.

BUY IN QUANTITY IF THE PRICE IS LOWER AND IF YOU CAN USE THAT QUANTITY.

Avoid waste caused by buying more than you can use. Not all large quantities are lower in price than smaller quantities. Check the arithmetic carefully. Usually staple foods and some clothing items, such as socks, have quantity discounts.

Now let us go from general rules to some specific areas of shopping.

When shopping for clothes, coordinate your purchases with your present wardrobe. Choose the right quality for your purpose. Do not put one hundred dollars into a party dress you are only going to wear once or twice a year. Put the most money into an outfit that you wear often.

Proper fit is absolutely essential for good appearance and comfort. It actually makes the garment last longer, too. Try garments on. If you order by mail, follow the directions for taking measurements suggested in the catalog or pattern book.

When having prescriptions filled, shop for prices by telephone. Pharmacies are required by law to tell you their prices. Ask your doctor for the generic term for the drug you need. Sometimes you can buy it for half the price of the brand names.

When buying furniture, check newspaper advertisements. Go to garage sales, rummage sales, and estate auctions. The best time to go is on a rainy day when things move slowly. The best buys at auctions come at the beginning and near the end.

Shop for furniture at independent stores. You can often bargain with an independent merchant. And do not be afraid to bargain. Merchants and salesmen expect you to do it for certain kinds of consumer goods such as cars, appliances, cameras, furniture, sporting goods, and some clothing. List prices for automobiles, for example, are the highest starting prices. You may secure price reductions also by bargaining for a higher price for your trade-in item or by securing more free services or extra accessories.

You can learn a great deal about buying a car if you take the time to read the advice given in an abundance of books and magazines. Here are some of the basic facts you should know.

American used cars are the best buy. If you are buying a truck, buy a new one if possible. Most truck owners put a lot of wear and tear on them. Some of them are run into the ground before they are traded.

Most cars sell five hundred to one thousand dollars below their "blue book" prices. Your credit union should have the list price (the price the dealer usually pays). Check your bank, too. Ask to see the invoice not the sticker price. Usually you can get the car for about one hundred fifty dollars over the invoice.

If a salesman leaves you in a room to discuss the deal with your partner, beware! Many offices are wired so the salesman can listen in to your conversation and find out how much you know and how badly you want the car. Take a walk around the block or, better yet, go home to talk it over.

If you know little about cars, take a class in auto mechanics. You may not want to fix the car yourself, but you will learn what repairs are and what they cost. Get a written estimate when you take your car to be repaired.

Learn to change your own oil. The price for oil in the store is half what it is in filling stations.

Remember! A bargain is a bargain if

• you really need what you buy
• the price is lower than usual for that item
• the price is lower than at nearby stores
• the item meets your needs in size, color, quality, and price.

GIVE GIFTS OF TIME AND TALENT

Because we live in a materialistic world, sooner or later most people find themselves overemphasizing money and possessions. We begin to use money as a standard criterion to judge a person's worth or the value of a gift without realizing we are doing it.

Perhaps your children hear you say, "The Whites are such a neat family. They've really got it made. Such a gorgeous house and everything else, too." As you talk your eyebrows go up, and the expression on your face says even more than your words. Your children get the message—having money and possessions means success and value.

Or you have just walked by the gift display at a wedding. On the way home you say, "Did you see what the Browns gave? It must have cost a fortune! What a gift!"

Or perhaps you fret about a gift you feel you must buy for a birthday or Christmas. When someone suggests something, you say, "Oh, I couldn't give them that. It's too chintzy. Why they must have paid twice as much for the gift they gave me last year!"

One family found it helpful to sit down together and make a list of all the experiences they could have that cost little or nothing. Their list included sitting by a blazing fire telling stories or listening to music; popping popcorn or making fudge; an outing at the river; a picnic in the park; attending coin, rock and gem, antique, and other kinds of hobby shows; tours of factories, historical sites, and art museums; and much more.

Last Father's Day Everett got some unusual gifts from the family. From Janeé he got three hand-made tickets "good for one anything." Also, he got from her a ticket lettered in red and blue on white background, which read, "Since Today is Your Day, Here is a quarter for the Jar." (The jar, decorated in red, white, and blue, sits on the kitchen counter. Each week one member of the family deposits a quarter. On July 4 the money goes for celebrating our country's birthday. It happened to be Everett's turn to put in the quarter.)

From Eric he received a handmade card and tickets good for one breakfast in bed and two hours of work. From Carla he got tickets for one garage sweeping, one patio sweeping, and one anything you want. From me he got tickets good for one shoeshine, one garden watering, and one anything; and three tickets good for one backrub.

"It's the greatest Father's Day I ever had," he declared.

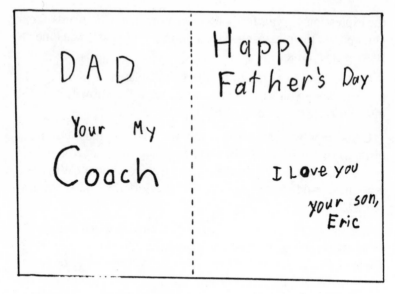

Eric's Fathers' Day card for his Dad.

Eric's gift.

Janeé's gift.

Many people appreciate services far more than most gifts money can buy. Babysitting, housecleaning, sewing, roofing, painting, running errands, and cutting hair are just a few of the gifts you can give. One woman bakes bread to give to newlyweds, together with a small recipe book she assembles from her own recipe file. A retired gentleman gives bulbs and cuttings from his garden with instructions on how to grow the plants.

Many times Christmas pushes over the cliff families who are tottering on the brink of bankruptcy. The Littles had been making valiant attempts at budgeting and managing, always keeping close to breaking even and yet periodically falling behind enough to need a loan or a readjustment of their debt load.

Then Christmas came. Besides spending the little extra cash Mr. Little had made doing odd jobs, they also went two hundred dollars into debt for presents. In March, unexpected doctor and drug bills came. In April, an insurance policy became due. Too many payments forced the Littles to borrow money again. This meant going deeper into a hole from which they could never emerge. Christmas gift giving had become a nightmare to them.

Unless your gifts are given in a spirit of love and within the limits of time and money you can afford, you should not give them. Meaningful giving requires thought and a certain amount of creativity.

When we were living in Germany, some German friends began building a house across the street from where we lived. We recorded each step of the building with our camera, beginning with the foundation and ending with the fertility celebration symbolized by a tree on top of the newly finished house. For Christmas we gave our new neighbors an album in which we had mounted the collection of pictures. When they opened the gift, they stood speechless with surprise and delight.

A macrame hanging, a needlepoint pillow, a picture, a game are all things you can make yourself. A father can build his little girl a dollhouse, his son a block car or truck.

The trick is to break the materialistic bond that keeps us thinking of gifts in terms of money. What could be more valuable to a child and parent, for example, than a gift of thirty minutes of time? Time and talent are our most precious possessions. When we give them to those we love, we give a little of ourselves.

A father gave his daughters, Jenny and Becky, coupons worth thirty minutes of his time. At dinner a few days later he was surprised to find a certificate from Becky beside his plate. She had given him a gift of time also.

A father and daughter's gifts of time:

Becky is super!

This coupon is worth 30 minutes of my time to spend with you.

I love you!

Daddy is superdooper!
Here is a certificat for any time you want to spend with me
I love you,
Becky

BARTER GOODS AND SERVICES

Barter simply means the exchange of goods and/or services without the use of money. From the beginning of time people have traded goods and services. Farmers traded wheat for lumber, eggs for sugar, hides for shoes, and so on.

Today many people ignore this profitable medium of exchange. Those who do not are finding it enables them to stretch their dollars far beyond what others on their income level can do.

John, a cabinetmaker, has built cupboards and cabinets for nearly all his many friends. He builds them in his spare time. In return, he has had the wiring done in his house, his car repaired, a calf butchered and cut up for his freezer, fishing flies handmade for him, and his will drawn up by a lawyer.

Perhaps you do not earn a living with a skill you consider tradeable. John is not a cabinetmaker by trade. Cabinetmaking is his hobby—something he enjoys very much. You undoubtedly have skills or perhaps a hobby that produces something desirable to others. When I was going to college, I wrote letters for a friend who knew little English, and she did my mending in return. Nearly everyone has some skill he can trade with someone else. You may be a great baker, and your neighbor may specialize in sewing.

Long ago when people got together to help a neighbor build his house, few of them were carpenters by trade. Imagine the money we would save today if we helped each other build our houses or even reroof or repaint them.

In Kathie's neighborhood the women get together to exchange clothes. They sit in a circle, hold up one item at a time and exchange. Another group, to which we belong, exchanges grocery coupons and at Christmas time has cookie exchanges.

One summer Kathie had in her seven-week summer class a young woman who changed dramatically during the course. Her husband, Bob, found out that the Lidens had just gotten a $3,300 estimate for putting forced-air heating and air conditioning into their house. He happened to be in that business. He was so grateful for the change in his wife that he was anxious to do something for the Lidens, and he offered to show Dave how to install the heating and air conditioning himself. It cost the Lidens $1,700 instead of the $3,300 they would have had to spend without Bob's help.

While Bob worked with Dave on the house, Kathie showed his wife, Ann, how to wallpaper. She also shared grocery shopping tips with Ann and helped her arrange a spice cabinet.

Dave helped another friend, who is a building contractor, with his surveying problems. That friend helped the Lidens install a new bathtub in their home and also helped them build a laundry room.

You might want to stage a neighborhood barter event. You and your friends could get together and exchange clothing, baby furniture, kitchen supplies, or anything else you might want to trade.

Remember, money not spent is worth more than additional income. The $1,600 the Lidens saved on air conditioning was actually worth $1,920 in additional earned income. Bartering can help you hang onto the money on which you have already paid taxes. It does not put you into a higher tax bracket. Here is a tax shelter that even middle-income people can afford.

SCUTTLE BILLS WITH SKILLS

Another good way to stretch the family dollar is to use each partner's skills as often as possible to eliminate the necessity of spending money for labor. Labor costs have skyrocketed. The man who cuts his sons' hair, mows his lawn, and fixes his leaky faucet has channeled the high cost of that labor into his own pocket, thereby stretching his dollars immeasurably.

Let us think of the many ways you can "do it yourself" and save those precious dollars. One of the best is to grow as much of your own food as possible. Another way is to replace clothes with permanent-press fabrics and washable knits and woolens, so that you can wash nearly everything yourself and avoid costly cleaning bills. Sew your own clothes and do your own mending and altering. If you do not know how, you can learn by attending an adult night class.

Learn to paint and wallpaper your house. Simple carpentry, plumbing, and repair will keep your house in good order. If you do not know how to repair something in your house, you can get help from the many simple books written for nonexperts like you. Here are three: *The Complete Home Handyman's Guide*, edited by Hubbard Cobb; *The New York Times Complete Manual of Home Repair* by Bernard Gladstone; and *Amateur Builder's Handbook* by Hubbard Cobb.

Make your own gifts. A little time spent at the library looking through crafts magazines should give you many ideas for gifts you can make. Night classes are another good place to learn skills you can use to make useful gifts. Egg decorating, ceramics, woodcraft, macrame, beading, jewelry making, needlepoint, knitting, crocheting, photography, and leathercraft are just a few possibilities.

Have a gift shelf or box somewhere in your house to keep gifts you make or buy throughout the year. Always be on the lookout for gifts for your family and friends. Then when their birthdays come—or Christmas—you will already have something to give them.

"Do it yourself" can save a great deal of money in food, too. For example, taking your lunch to work instead of buying it or baking your own bread and pastries can save money.

Using skills to stretch your income is an indispensable element of thrift. A marriage motivated by an attitude of thrift will have no trouble with finances unless a partner falls into a devastating money trap.

Avoid Money Pitfalls

You can be the smartest shopper in your neighborhood, put more emphasis on character than on cash, exchange goods and services with your friends, and use your skills to save money, and still find yourself in trouble if you do not know how to avoid five major money pitfalls.

IMPULSE SPENDING

The first and most common pitfall is impulse spending. To

make your money finance your partnership adequately, you must exorcise the most powerful enemy of any family-spending plan—that demon, impulse buying.

The biggest money loss experienced by families happens through a host of small purchases that most people make without really being aware of them (the charming little angel filled with cologne, for example, that sits on the dresser after its purchase from the Avon lady, unused and untouched).

There is nothing wrong with buying cosmetics you know you like, but spending money on something new without trying it first or simply because you cannot resist the cuteness of the bottle will drain hundreds of dollars from your limited funds and may cost a vacation trip you would have enjoyed far more.

Shopping has become a popular American pastime. Many of us, if we have nothing better to do, drive to the nearest shopping center to shop. We go not to buy any particular thing, but just to look and enjoy ourselves. Children are brought up to believe that shopping is a form of entertainment. They tuck a few dollars into their purses or pockets, find a friend, and go shopping.

If you want to remove the temptation to shop impulsively, never go shopping without a list of specific things to buy. Make it a point to tell your dimes, quarters, and dollars where to go, instead of asking where they went.

Trying to follow an unrealistically austere plan can dump you even deeper into the pitfall of impulse buying, so be sensible. Ron and Susie made the mistake of setting up an unrealistic money plan. Their strict budget became a vise as they tried to pay off debts too fast. They ate hamburger and noodles day after day. They did not buy clothes, go bowling, or take a trip. Shopping centers were off limits. Finally, they both had an impulse to splurge on the same day. In one shopping spree, they completely nullified the weeks of sacrifice and austerity.

Many people make the same mistake as Ron and Susie. They live frugally for months. Suddenly they cannot stand it any longer, so they go on a spending binge, buying the clothes they have long needed, the tennis rackets they have long wanted, and they top it off with a thirty-dollar evening on the town. All on credit, of course.

Be especially wary of impulse buying when you decide to buy a bigger item such as a washing machine or a car. If you plan to buy a washing machine, for example, go to the library and use *Consumer Reports* to check the ratings on each brand of machine.

Ask yourself what you want this machine to do for you. Remember, the more buttons there are to push, the more there is to go wrong. Take a cue from the businessman again. When he plans to purchase a new item, he gets bids. In your case, you get prices.

For one month clip from newspapers the advertisements and prices of the washing machines that interest you. When you go to the store, you know what you want, and you know what you can get it for. Never let a salesman pressure you into impulse buying by telling you this is the last time you can get such a deal at this giveaway price. There is always tomorrow and another deal, probably better than the first.

EXCESSIVE CREDIT BUYING

A second trap beckoning eager consumers is excessive credit buying. Credit can be an effective money management tool when used wisely. "In light of inflation," says Dr. Richard Morse, a family economist at Kansas State University, "to pay cash and never borrow money is stupid."[1]

But it takes skill to use credit wisely. Never allow your loans to exceed twenty percent of your annual take-home pay. And shop for credit just as you would shop for other valuable commodities.

The best source of credit is to borrow against your own savings account. One family actually lends money to themselves from their own savings account. They set up a repayment schedule, giving themselves the eighteen percent a year interest they would have paid had they borrowed on a standard credit card. Thus, they benefit from their borrowing.

Another excellent source of money is a loan on insurance. If you have paid on your life insurance long enough, it has a loan, or surrender, value. You can borrow up to the amount of the loan value at a reasonable interest rate. You may pay it back any way you wish. You pay interest on the loan until it is paid off. In the event of death, the balance of the loan is subtracted from the face value.

You can also borrow money at banks or credit unions for less than most credit card loans. Avoid small loan companies unless you are desperate enough to pay exceedingly high interest.

Try the thirty-, sixty-, and ninety- day credit plans offered by many department stores with their credit cards. You pay one-third of the total price each thirty, sixty, and ninety days with no interest.

Do not pay cash for a big purchase. Ask for a thirty-days with-no-interest account. Then if something goes wrong with the merchandise you can get quick action.

Here are general guidelines to help you avoid the excessive-debt money trap:

Under certain circumstances it is reasonable to borrow:
1. To cover unavoidable financial emergencies
2. To meet a major need for a durable item or to pay for something sure to provide lasting benefits.

Under other circumstances, do not borrow:
1. When you may not be able to repay
2. To finance a life-style beyond your means (a fancy vacation, dinner out)
3. To support impulse buying
4. For an enterprise with an element of risk
5. When you already have as much debt as you can handle.

INSUFFICIENT SAVINGS

A third pitfall to avoid is insufficient savings. The key to saving is to save something regularly even if it is a small amount. If you begin with as little as five dollars a week, at the end of the first year you will have your first nest egg of $260. Some people find that if they start small, they can gradually increase the proportion of their savings until they finally reach the recommended ten percent of their net income.

Treat savings as an expense, and budget for it just as you would any other expense. Every family should have an emergency fund equal to at least two months' income. This fund should be kept in a readily accessible place such as a savings account.

If a woman does not work, it is wise to keep the family emergency fund in a savings account in her name. Then it serves the dual purpose of covering unexpected expenses and providing cash for her in the event of her husband's death when joint accounts might be sealed.

LIVING ON THE WRONG INCOME LEVEL

A fourth trap is living on the wrong income level: too much house, too much automobile, too many expensive clothes, and so on.

Harry and Linda Tait found just the house they wanted on five acres in the country. It was built on a hill and had a gorgeous view in three directions. The land was undeveloped. No barn or stable. No trees. No landscaping.

Harry and Linda could barely afford the house at $58,000—$340 a month after down payment. The house would cost far more money than the Taits could ever suspect. Putting the well into good working condition, landscaping, planting trees and a garden, and building a stable were all costs they could ill afford. Many couples find themselves in this same plight, struggling to finance day-to-day living while supporting too much house.

Too much automobile can cause the same kind of problem. Few people realize that, next to the family home, the automobile is the largest single drain on family finances. We spend more than $75 billion annually to pay for it and for the gasoline, taxes, parts, accessories, and insurance it requires. No one knows how much we pay for service, repairs, and incidentals.

The cost of a car includes much more than the cost of buying it. Some families decide to keep the old car instead of trading it in when it comes time to get a newer one. They believe they now have a second car for practically nothing, but operating a second car greatly increases transportation costs. You still must buy insurance, tires, and batteries, plus the extra gas your old car probably consumes. You will be driving more miles simply because you can.

Some families need a new car. Others merely want "wheels." Economy model cars have the same wheelbase and same chassis as many of the deluxe models, but with a lot of things left off. If you simply want transportation, you can get along without the automatic transmission, tinted glass, power steering, and a great deal of chrome. The important thing is to buy only as much car as you can afford.

Keeping up with fashion every year may be a costly habit, and one you cannot afford. Men and women alike can fall into the trap of overspending on clothes. Budget for clothes just as you budget for your other expenses. Then follow the advice given under how to shop for clothes.

DEPENDING TOO MUCH ON A SECOND INCOME

The last of the five major money traps is depending too much on a second income. Doing this can bring a family to disaster if the wife becomes pregnant or for some other reason can no longer contribute to family earnings. Most money experts advise families to plan to use the wife's earnings for the less critical items on the budget and never depend on them when deciding how much debt you can handle.

Families will find other pitfalls to rob them of their money and wreck their money plans, but these are the most common. If you can avoid them and at the same time develop an attitude of thrift, you will stretch your dollars far beyond your wildest dreams.

Hebrews 13:5-6 gives us this encouragement: "Let your way of life be free from the love of money, being content with what you have; for He Himself has said, 'I WILL NEVER DESERT YOU, NOR WILL I EVER FORSAKE YOU.' so that we confidently say, 'THE LORD IS MY HELPER, I WILL NOT BE AFRAID.' "

9

Get the Most from Your Food Dollar

GAIN CONTROL OF MEAL PLANNING

Walk into any grocery store, and you will find grim-faced shoppers trying to provide nourishing food for their families, with a limited amount of money. In spite of the ever-increasing price of food, too many of us spend more than we have to for groceries.

To get the most from your food dollar you must invest time and effort in careful planning and shopping. Composing your shopping list and your weekly menu may take more time than doing the shopping. The first step is to gain recipe control.

Research experts tell us that we use only twenty percent of our filed recipes and repeat the same favorites eighty percent of the time. For the average household this means we cook about ten basic dishes year in and year out. If you are one of those people who would rather clip than cook, now is the time to take charge of yourself.

Find the courage to attack your pile of "wishful thinking." Set aside two hours and gather those recipe clippings out of the drawer or bulging recipe file. Go through them with a critical eye. If you know you will probably never try a certain recipe even if you live to be 100, throw it away.

To separate your recipes from "untried" to "kitchen tested," use two boxes or notebooks, whichever you prefer. One will contain untried recipes. Tested recipes go in the other. Tape the recipes on five-by-seven-inch index cards, if using the boxes, and file them under titled dividers until they are tested by the family. Then either toss them out or transfer them to the "kitchen tested" box. Use the same principle if using notebooks.

Imagine yourself the executive manager of the small food processing plant that serves the family to which you belong. Take inventory, incorporating unused portions of food into plans for the coming week. Suppose there is a small portion of last night's Swiss steak, some hamburger left over from tacos, and an assortment of leftover vegetables. Put these together. Add any vegetable water you have saved, a can of bouillon, and a can of tomatoes. Season, and you have a hearty vegetable soup.

To avoid repeating the same task every time I plan menus, I created my own menu planner notebook. In it I listed and numbered favorite menus. As I try new things the family likes, I add them to the list. Through the years I have accumulated more than seventy different menus. When doing my planning, I simply flip through the book, choose the menus for the week, and put those numbers on the family calendar along with any new ideas created from leftovers.

As you plan your menu, look at each food critically. Ask yourself some hard questions:

• What foods are most important to my family?
• How does the price of the foods I have chosen compare with the price of other foods that could replace them?
• Will my family eat and enjoy what I have planned?
• Have I included any foods that have empty calories, such as soda pop, potato chips, or sugar-coated cereal?

Many people use menu planners like this one. Make a master copy, and then have it duplicated at a quick-print shop.

	Sunday	Monday	Tuesday	Wednesday	Thursday	Friday	Saturday
b r e a k f a s t							
l u n c h							
d i n n e r							
s n a c k s							

Make your shopping list based on planned menus plus whatever you need to replenish stock. This simplifies shopping. Stick to your list and avoid impulse buying. Surveys show you spend fifty cents a minute on impulse buying when you linger in a store more than thirty minutes, so get what you came for and get out fast!

It is best to leave very young children at home and never shop for groceries when you are hungry. If you do take your children, take advantage of the opportunity to teach them shopping skills.

BE A BETTER BUYER

Supermarkets are to many shoppers what beautiful spider webs are to many flies. Retailers spend a great deal of money to learn what colors calm you down or excite you as you walk through the well-planned aisles. Music regulates your mood. Every supermarket has about ten thousand items displayed to encourage you to reach out and put them into your shopping cart. This is a place to go only when you have to. When you do, know what you are doing and pray for self-control!

Where you do your shopping affects your grocery bill. Check

prices at nearby stores, study advertisements, and learn what each store in your area charges for specific items. Make price checking a family project. Assign different areas of food to each member of the family. One person can be responsible for meat and dairy products, another for vegetables, fruit, beverages, and so on. Keep records of spending and records for each store. Talk about your findings on family night.

Allow part of your grocery money for stock. Over a period of two or three months you will probably find specials on most of the items you need. The idea is to choose your shopping times. Buy replacement items only when they are on sale.

By shopping carefully, buying when the price is right, and buying in quantity you can save ten to twenty percent on everything you buy. On many spices sold in large quantities in natural food stores, you can save from three hundred to five hundred percent over the cost of the little cans of spices you buy in the supermarket. A two-pound can of yeast is sixteen times cheaper than the small packets. This only pays if you use the yeast or spice often enough to use it up before it deteriorates.

Get in the habit of reading unit pricing labels. This allows you to compare different size packages by determining the exact cost per unit measure. Suppose, for example, a six-ounce can of something is twenty-nine cents and a thirteen-ounce can is sixty cents. Which is cheaper? The unit price label will tell you the cost per pound of each item—seventy-seven cents for the six-ounce size and seventy-four cents for the thirteen-ounce size. If the unit price is not given, figure it out for yourself.

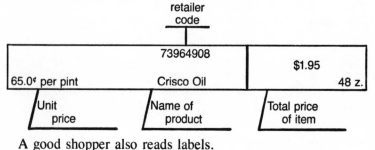

A good shopper also reads labels.

DID YOU KNOW?

- Ingredients are listed in order of volume in the product.
  ie: When sugar is listed first, that means there is more suga··
  than other ingredients in the product.
- Nutritional labeling is voluntary unless the product makes a
  dietary claim or is enriched.
- All additives are not listed on labels.
- Spices, flavorings, colorings can still be listed in a general way.
- Only dairy products are required by law to have dates which are
  not in code. These dates tell you when the product should be
  removed from the shelf.
- Preservatives must be listed with a statement about their purpose.
- Enriched means adding back vitamins and minerals to a standard level.
- Fortified means the product has had extra vitamins and minerals added.

WHAT DOES RDA MEAN?

U.S. Recommended daily Allowances are the amounts of protein,
vitamins and minerals that an adult should eat every day to keep
healthy.

- Nutrition labels list the RDA by percentage. To make sure you
  get enough vitamins and minerals, the percentage for each
  from different foods should add up to about 100 each day.
  Children have different needs.

HOW TO USE NUTRITION LABELS

- Nutrition information is per serving.
- Labels tell size of serving (1 cup etc.)
- Seven vitamins and minerals are shown in the same order on all
  nutrition labels.
- Use this information to plan more nutritious meals and get
  more nutrition for your food dollar.

A label may include optional listings for cholesterol, fats, and
sodium.

Reprinted by permission of Northern California Grocers' Association.

To shop wisely, you must know what convenience foods really cost. The more preparation that has gone into an item, the more you pay. Some of these work-saver foods are bargains, but others have a very high price and save you very little work. Learn to examine them critically.

Often you can find ways to substitute foods you can make yourself. A pound of dried apricots, for example, retails for approximately $2.50 a pound in food stores. You can purchase fresh apricots in season for about 25¢ a pound and use a dehydrator. Three pounds of fresh fruit will make a pound of dried fruit at a total cost of 77¢. If you grow your own fruits or vegetables, the cost is reduced to about two cents a pound for the dried product.

If you use a dehydrator to preserve fruits in season and vegetables from your garden, it will quickly pay for itself. Very few nutrients are lost in dehydration, so this is excellent equipment to use to help keep your family healthy.

Explore the possibility of sharing the cost of a dehydrator with another family. In fact, several families could use it, each growing and drying different foods to divide among the families involved. Sharing costs in this way will greatly reduce food bills.

Making your own yogurt is another example of an easy way to save money. For a starter always use a good dry or unflavored commercial yogurt that is made with lactobacillus Bulgaricus culture. Every month or so use a fresh starter.

To make yogurt with noninstant dried milk, mix in blender three cups warm water (105°-110°) and one cup dried milk. Add one-fourth cup yogurt starter (room temperature) and a bit of vanilla. Pour into containers and make in your usual manner. This yogurt will set in three to four hours.

Make yogurt ice cream, Popsicles, dips, and dressings. Replace sour cream or buttermilk by mixing equal amounts of water and yogurt in blender. Get some good recipes and experiment. You will like it.

Other things that are simple to do yourself:
Baked goods. Compare the cost of the ingredients for your favor-

ite recipes with bakery products. Usually you can make them more cheaply yourself.

Dr. Clive M. McCay and his associates at Cornell University developed a formula to increase nutrients in your packaged mixes or your own cake, bread, and cookie recipes. Cornell formula: For each cup of flour called for by your recipe, first place in your measuring cup:

> 1 T. soy flour
> 1 T. nonfat dry milk powder
> 1 T. wheat germ
> Fill the remainder of the cup with flour.[1]

Cereals. See chapter 10 for instructions for making your own.

Corn chips. Slice, fry, and salt a package of corn tortillas.

Chives. Use chopped green onion tops.

Lunch meats. Figure the price of this meat per pound, and you will see how extravagant you are to buy it. Instead, buy a large ham or grind meat for lunch spreads. Use eggs mixed with mayonnaise, too. For something different, mix creamed cheese with jars of strained baby food meat to get a sandwich filling that costs approximately seventy-five cents and makes about ten sandwiches.

Syrup. Pour one cup of boiling water over two cups of sugar. Boil two minutes. Add one-half teaspoon maple flavoring.

Sauces. White sauce you make costs one-fifth as much as prepared white sauce mixes. It is simple and quick, so take the time to learn to make it yourself. To get rid of unwanted lumps easily, beat the mixture with an egg beater or wire whip. You can also save money by making your own curry sauce (all you need to add is a little curry powder), taco sauce, tartar sauce, and sauce for vegetables. Add a few spices to oil and vinegar mixed on a ratio of one part vinegar to three parts oil, and save the cost of prepared salad dressing.

Crumbs and stuffing. Make your own by saving all end slices and stale bread. Bake them at low temperature and roll them in a brown paper bag. You can make your own stuffing mix by adding sage and thyme. You will pay only one-sixteenth the cost of prepared stuffing—a whopping big savings for a better product.

MIXES

Rice pilaf is notoriously high priced for the amount of work it takes to prepare. All you do to make pilaf is cook rice in chicken broth with whatever you wish to add, such as onions. Making it yourself costs one-fourth as much as buying a packaged mix.

Homemade hash browns cost one-fifth the cost of the packaged variety, and you save more than two-thirds the price if you scallop your own potatoes. You can make your own macaroni and cheese for one-half the cost of a mix and one-fourth the cost of the frozen product. Most add-to-hamburger mixes cost twice as much as your homemade version of these dishes.

MEAT

Cut your own meat if cut meat is more expensive. You can cut beef stew chunks from pot roasts. Cut some slices for steaks from a large roast of top sirloin or an eye of round. Buy a whole loin of pork if it is "on special," and cut into one or two roasts. Cut the remaining loin into chops. Many butchers will cut large pieces of meat to your specifications. Cut up your own chickens.

When buying meat, look for the cuts that provide the most cooked lean for the money spent. Use small servings, and rely on more economical foods to fill in meals. Red meat should not be served more than three or four times a week. Use alternatives such as eggs, beans, peas, peanut butter, cheese, and grains as well as fish and poultry.

You can also use meat extenders such as TVP (Texturized Vegetable Protein) and grain. Derived from soybeans, TVP can be used to extend tuna, chicken, and hamburger.

Buy fresh fluid milk at a food or retail dairy store in half- or one-gallon containers. Usually smaller sizes are a few cents higher. Home-delivered milk usually costs more. Use nonfat dry milk in cooking and as a beverage extender. Buy it in as large a package as you can store and use without waste.

Buy fruits and vegetables in season. Prices of canned, frozen, and dehydrated fruits and vegetables vary widely by item, brand, grade, type of process, and seasoning. Look for vegetables and fruits that supply the most nourishment for the lowest price.

Try lower-priced brands of food. You may like them just as well as the expensive ones.

Packaging is costly. When you buy raisins, for example, buy them in large boxes. If you want them packaged for lunches, do it yourself with plastic wrap.

To become a smart shopper takes a little effort, but once you realize the importance of saving nickles and dimes you will find them multiplying into quarters and dollars. Best of all you will provide better nourishment for smaller cost.

BUY IN BULK

You can save even more by using a buddy system and buying some of your food in bulk. Here is how it worked for the Lidens.

They joined a group of Christians and formed a co-op. They educated each other in the biblical seven grains: wheat, oats, corn, rye, barley, rice, and soybeans. This group found out where local markets bought fresh produce and asked if the wholesale distributors would sell to individuals. The answer was, "Yes." They would be happy to sell to anyone in case lots.

The group learned that restaurant suppliers will often sell to anyone with an order of $200 or more. The co-op could buy oil, yeast, and even pans at big savings. They made up a list of wholesalers and factories and formed telephone chains to arrange for splitting fresh foods and case items.

You, too, can begin a search for bulk suppliers. To locate wheat go to your United States Department of Agriculture office or the local county extension-service agent. They can usually suggest a good supplier and tell you where to have the grain tested for protein and moisture content if the supplier cannot give you that information.

If you know someone at a bakery, ask where the bakery buys its wheat. Ask at feed stores or grain mills. Nutrition teachers at local colleges may be able to help. Health food stores may provide you with the information you want.

Finding powdered noninstant milk can be a problem. Your best bet is to call a local supplier of dairy products. Check the milk carton in your refrigerator to see if the supplier is local. If not, check the Yellow Pages for one who is.

For dehydrated foods, call the Scouts office in your city. They usually have a list of suppliers for camping trips.

To find fresh produce write your chamber of commerce. Some state governments have a directory of manufacturers and producers. Check the farm bureau and any college agricultural departments.

Compiling a list of wholesalers does take time, but it pays off in the long run. Do not get discouraged, and good hunting!

Use Foods High in Value—Low in Cost

Look for leaks in your food budget. Empty calories cost money and give you nothing. At our house we need to eliminate cereals that go up in cost as routinely as Tuesday follows Monday.

Changing my family's breakfast habits has been difficult, but we have discovered a book that has been helpful. It is called *The Good Breakfast Book* and was written by Nikki and David Goldbeck.

If you want to change your family's breakfast habits, several choices are open to you. You may have main dishes such as broiled steak, liver, or fish; egg dishes; cheese dishes; and so on. Instead of cooking it yourself, have everything ready to go the night before. Then each person can cook his own breakfast when he needs to eat it. This suggestion is for families like ours having staggered hours in the morning. If you have a main dish for breakfast, a light meal will do at night.

Another way of adding protein to breakfast is to serve a high protein drink. Add brewer's yeast to a glass of fruit juice or water. Begin with one teaspoon of yeast flakes and work up to a tablespoonful. You must start out small, or you will blow up like a balloon.

Make up your own drink. If you have a blender, toss in a number of ingredients such as granular lecithin, powdered protein, wheat germ, honey, an egg, fruit, and skim milk or fruit juice. Or use yogurt and milk as a base for adding fruit and high protein ingredients.

Do not expect this drink to taste delicious. You may have to acquire a taste for it, but even if it tastes like medicine, the extra energy it will give you will be well worth the effort it takes to get it down.

Your third option is to try the low cost grain cereals suggested in chapter 10—cracked wheat, whole wheat berries, or rice served with sugar, cinnamon, or raisins. Make your own granola, too, and use it as topping on ice cream and yogurt. Mix it into cookies.

Cereals that offer the most food value for the least cost are the whole grain cereals you cook, such as rolled oats, toasted or cracked wheat, and unrefined cornmeal. (Remember that instant cereals generally cost twice as much as the quick-cooking types.) Next best are the milled enriched cereals that you cook, such as farina, cream of rice, and degermed cornmeal.

If you simply cannot break the cold-cereal habit, take a look at some charts comparing the nutritional value of various cereals. Then refuse to buy all cereals high in sugar and low in food value.

Of the ready-to-eat cereals, the best values are those with the least amount of sugar and fat, those made with whole grains, and those that have added nutritional ingredients such as soy, dry milk, wheat germ, bran, and raisins.

To save more money and provide a nutritious "meal in a dish," serve homemade soup at least once a week. Serve it with fruit salad and whole wheat bread.

It takes time to prepare soup, but, if you make a big pot, you can freeze what you do not use and have a fast easy meal the next time.

Here are some suggestions for making and storing soup:

- Freeze in jars—leave some air space.
- Soup with vegetables and grains costs about seven cents a cup. With meat, eleven cents.
- Use knuckle, shank, or neck bones for beef stock. Add one

tablespoon of vinegar to draw out the calcium and other minerals. The vinegar will evaporate with the odor after cooking.

- Add more usable protein to your vegetable soups. Use one-fourth to one-half pound browned hamburger or other cooked meat. Make a master mix of equal amounts of dry green split peas, pearl barley, lentils, and brown rice. Store in airtight containers. Add one cup of soup mix to approximately eight cups of liquid soup base (water, tomato, beef stock). Simmer 1½ hours and then add vegetables and cook until tender-crisp.
- Slow cookers are excellent for making soup.
- Do not forget about cream-base soups.

    Mix 3 to 4 cups of milk to 1½ to 2 cups cooked vegetables. Add a little salt and butter to flavor and 1 to 2 tablespoonfuls of flour to thicken. Try celery with 1 tablespoonful of chopped onion, or how about potatoes, 1 tablespoonful chopped onion and parsley, and 3 tablespoonfuls of chopped celery. Add rice to soup to increase the usable protein.

- Dry or freeze celery tops for soups.
- Keep a quart jar in freezer and pop in leftover vegetables for soup making. Use in one month for better flavor.

Spend time planning food combinations to decrease your cost and upgrade your diet. Mix and match grains, milk products, seeds, and legumes (a small amount of complete proteins such as eggs, milk, and cheese should be eaten at the same meal).

If you serve chow mein (bean sprouts and fried rice) using three-fourths cup of beans plus two cups of rice, you increase the protein forty-three percent. This would compare to the protein in a 9½-ounce steak.

Examples of how protein content may be increased:

Protein	Protein Increase If Combined	Example
¾ c. beans +		
2 c. rice	43%	Chow mein
¼ c. beans +		

1½ c. whole flour	33%	Tostados
¼ c. beans +		
1 c. cornmeal	50%	Chili and cornbread
1 c. soy flour +		
4 c. whole wheat flour	32%	Bread, waffles
½ c. soy flour +		
3¼ c. whole wheat flour +		
½ c. seeds	42%	Bread, cakes
4 slices whole wheat bread,		
or ¾ c. macaroni,		Cheese sandwich, or
and 1 oz. cheese	25%	macaroni/cheese
⅓ c. dry milk +		
1 lb. potatoes	7%	Scalloped potatoes

Seeds include sunflower and ground sesame seeds.
You can use cheese or yogurt in place of milk.

Another excellent way to increase food value at low cost is to turn grains into nutritious vegetables by sprouting them. You can easily turn your kitchen into an indoor garden, and you will get a crop in two to seven days, regardless of the weather.

The easiest, most reliable, and most appetizing sprouts to grow are alfalfa, bean, chia, cress, fenugreek, mustard, lentil, radish, rye, and wheat. Use only untreated seeds sold for growing purposes. These seeds are alive, and you can expect a high percentage of germination. Legumes and grains sold in food markets may be dead and therefore will not sprout. Seeds treated with insecticide-fungicide mixtures can be poisonous. Most natural food, or health food, stores stock grains, nuts, and legumes suitable for sprouting.

Select seeds of good quality. Check for discoloration, breaks, cracks, and other imperfections. Dead or damaged seeds can ferment, causing any good seed you have to decay also.

To sprout alfalfa, for example, use a pint or quart jar. Add one teaspoon of seeds and cover with lukewarm water. Place a piece of clean nylon stocking over the top and put a rubber band around the lip of the jar to hold it secure. Turn the jar upside down and

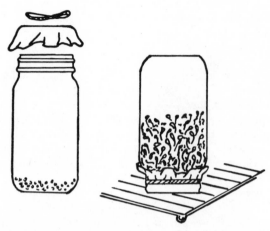

place on cake rack to drain off moisture. Put the jar on the rack in a dark cabinet. Drain and rinse every morning and night.

When seeds pop, put leafy green sprouts in artificial light or indirect sunlight for a couple of hours until the leaves become green. This increases the chlorophyll content of the leaves. Lentils, rye, and wheat can grow in light or dark. Keep mung beans and fenugreek dark and water often. Use mung sprouts when they are one-fourth- to one-inch long.

Sprouts have the most nutrients and taste best if you use them soon after they reach mature size. Rinse off loose seed hulls or use hulls and all. If you must store sprouts, store loosely in an airtight container in the refrigerator. Do not use plastic bags, because the delicate sprouts tend to get crushed, and damaged sprouts are quick to decay. Properly stored, sprouts will keep a few days to a week.

You can add sprouts, at the last minute, to butter-steamed vegetables or use them in sandwiches, on crackers, or in salads. They are also good in bread and pilaf. They will add flavor and texture as well as an abundance of nutrients.

GARDENING BRINGS BONUSES

By growing as much of your own food as possible you can accomplish two important objectives. You provide an uncontaminated food source, and you save many dollars.

In America, where we are used to acres and acres of land, we may overlook the many places available to us for growing food. If you have fences, train grapes, berries, or beans to grow beside them. Strawberries make excellent ground cover and give a tasty treat as well. Instead of useless shade trees, plant nut or fruit trees for shade. Their blossoms in the spring add beauty to your yard.

You can grow a lot of food in very small spaces, as shown in the books *Postage Stamp Gardening* and *The Apartment Farmer,* both written by Duane Newcomb. The money return for dollars spent is high.

If you purchase all your seed, fertilizers, and equipment, a garden will cost you approximately $10 to $12 per adult and $5 or $6 per child, with a dollar return of $134 to $150 per adult and $60 to $75 per child. There is no way to place a value on the fact that your own food can be free of chemicals.

You can save even more by using table scraps, straw, wood ashes, and other natural materials for fertilizer. Put your table scraps in a blender, add a pinch of yeast, fill with water, and liquefy. This will give you instant compost for your garden.

Ask a friend who gardens about his favorite books, plant nursery, and secrets of success. If you are new to an area, talk to your local county agriculture agent about what is adaptable to your specific location. In your priority notebook jot down the dates of the approximate time of the last frost in the spring and the first frost in the fall.

While you are exploring gardening ideas, start a compost pile to lighten the soil and revitalize it. Place a wire fence around your compost pile and toss in grass clippings, shredded leaves, manure, and table scraps. This dumping ground becomes rich mulch and fertilizer. About a month before the last frost is expected you may cultivate your garden spot and get ready for the big event.

A loving caretaker of plants and a wise cook can change the eating habits of the next generation. So swap ideas and plants. Build over the back fence a friendship that promotes eating well, feeling great, and having fun!

FOOD STORAGE—PRACTICAL, PALATABLE, AND PRUDENT

Have you ever walked into a supermarket only to find rows of empty shelves? For a variety of reasons, more and more people have had this experience in recent years.

During the Cuban crisis in the early 1960s, President Kennedy's simple statement that every home should have a two-week food supply caused panic in cities such as Los Angeles and emptied supermarket shelves within hours.

Military personnel who live overseas often find commissary shelves missing many important items. Strikes also reduce grocery store stock in an alarmingly short time.

To prepare for possible disasters is only one of the many reasons food storage is a must for every smooth-running home. Other reasons include preparation for personal emergencies such as accidents, illness, or unemployment. Dave Liden was able to go into business for himself because his family had a storage program and would not need to buy food for at least six months.

Food storage also provides a hedge against inflation. One man bought fifty pounds of coffee for a dollar a pound when he heard about the failure of the Brazilian coffee crop. By doing this he saved over one hundred fifty dollars. The Lidens can still make bread for nine cents a loaf, because they bought their wheat several years ago.

Buying food for storage when it is sale priced reduces the food budget. Because you have staples stored, you have money to buy greater quantities of specially priced food.

The following are some general guidelines for storing food. Consider the basic food groups: milk and milk products, meat and meat substitutes, fruits and vegetables, breads and cereals. From each group, select foods that your family needs and is used to eating. Then store what you eat and eat what you store.

Take an inventory of what you have on hand. From it make a list of what you need, using some kind of system to establish priority. Five basic items are wheat, sugar, milk, salt, and vitamin tablets.

HOME CARE OF PURCHASED FROZEN FOODS

Suggested Maximum Home-Storage Periods To Maintain Good Quality in Purchased Frozen Foods

Food	Approximate holding period at 0° F	Food	Approximate holding period at 0° F
Fruits and vegetables		**Meat—Continued**	
Fruits:	*Months*		*Months*
Cherries	12	Cooked meat:	
Peaches	12	Meat dinners	3
Raspberries	12	Meat pie	3
Strawberries	12	Swiss steak	3
Fruit juice concentrates:			
Apple	12	**Poultry**	
Grape	12	Chicken:	
Orange	12	Cut-up	9
Vegetables:		Livers	3
Asparagus	8	Whole	12
Beans	8	Duck, whole	6
Cauliflower	8	Goose, whole	6
Corn	8	Turkey:	
Peas	8	Cut-up	6
Spinach	8	Whole	12
		Cooked chicken and turkey:	
Baked goods		Chicken or turkey dinners	
Bread and yeast rolls:		(sliced meat and gravy)	6
White bread	3	Chicken or turkey pies	6
Cinnamon rolls	2	Fried chicken	4
Plain rolls	3	Fried chicken dinners	4
Cakes:			
Angel	2	**Fish and shellfish**	
Chiffon	2	Fish:	
Chocolate layer	4	Fillets:	
Fruit	12	Cod, flounder, haddock,	
Pound	6	halibut, pollack	6
Yellow	6	Mullet, ocean perch, sea	
Danish pastry	3	trout, striped bass	3
Doughnuts:		Pacific Ocean perch	2
Cake type	3	Salmon steaks	2
Yeast raised	3	Sea trout, dressed	3
Pies (unbaked):		Striped bass, dressed	3
Apple	8	Whiting, drawn	4
Boysenberry	8	Shellfish:	
Cherry	8	Clams, shucked	3
Peach	8	Crabmeat:	
		Dungeness	3
Meat		King	10
Beef:		Oysters, shucked	4
Hamburger or chipped (thin)		Shrimp	12
steaks	4	Cooked fish and shellfish:	
Roasts	12	Fish with cheese sauce	3
Steaks	12	Fish with lemon butter sauce	3
Lamb:		Fried fish dinner	3
Patties (ground meat)	4	Fried fish sticks, scallops, or	
Roasts	9	shrimp	3
Pork, cured	2	Shrimp creole	3
Pork, fresh:		Tuna pie	3
Chops	4		
Roasts	8	**Frozen desserts**	
Sausage	2	Ice cream	1
Veal:		Sherbert	1
Cutlets, chops	9		
Roasts	9		

U.S. Department of Agriculture, Home and Garden Bulletin No. 69

The lowest temperature short of freezing should be used for storing most foods. Temperatures from forty to sixty degrees are best. Temperature should not exceed seventy degrees. Do not store food near heating ducts, furnaces, hot water pipes, or other heat sources. Keep everything six inches off cement. Keep supplies in cool, dry, dark places.

Rotate supplies. Place new supplies behind old ones and do not forget to label all containers, indicating contents and date of purchase.

Dried fruits should be as dry as possible. Pack loosely in clean glass fruit jars. Place without lids in the oven and heat for twenty minutes at 150 degrees, then cap.

Canned goods purchased from markets should be turned over each three to six months. Maximum storage is two to three years. Discard any bulged or leaking cans without tasting the product.

What you store is as individual as each family's eating habits. It may help to look at a list of suggested items to keep on hand. Adapt this list to your own needs, making a note of how much you have on hand.

Possible Storage Items

basic cookbook	canned/dried vegetables
storage containers	variety of dried legumes
wheat	kidney beans
white flour	pinto beans
nonfat dried milk	navy beans
sugar/honey	soybeans
salt/pepper	lentils
yeast	peas
baking soda	variety of grains
baking powder	rice
shortening	oats
oil	rye
peanut butter	barley

corn
canned/dried fruit
canned sauces (tomato)
canned meats/TVP
margarine/butter
soup
vinegar
vanilla
vitamin/mineral tablets
vitamin C
bouillon cubes
chocolate/carob
canned milk
macaroni
salad dressings
cornmeal
raisins
gelatin
pickles/olives
catsup
herbs/spices
soy sauce
Worcestershire sauce
dried onion
coffee/tea (herb teas)
aluminum foil

plastic wrap/bags
paper cups/plates
paper towels/napkins
light bulbs
toothpicks
shoelaces
string/rope
stationery supplies
candles/matches
bottled water
ammonia
laundry/hand/dish soap
bleach
toilet tissue
razor blades
sanitary napkins
toothpaste/toothbrush
shampoo
flashlight/batteries
hand can opener
bottle opener
needles/thread/scissors
blankets
transistor radio
first aid kit/home and car
wheat grinder

The United States Government makes available certain helpful publications. Write for a current price list and then order by title and number.

	Office of Communication U.S. Department of Agriculture Washington, D.C. 20250		
		Order	No.
Family Fare: A Guide to Good Nutrition		G	1
Freezing Combination Main Dishes		G	40
Vegetables in Family Meals: A Guide for Consumers		G	105
Keeping Food Safe to Eat: A Guide for Homemakers		G	162
Your Money's Worth in Foods		G	183

Knowing how to stretch your food dollar and increase your knowledge is really a matter of self-education for each family. Write for the Consumer Information Catalog and look into the Consumer Information Center's low-cost bulletins.

Consumer Information Center Pueblo, CO 81009		
Home and Garden Bulletin No.	**Title**	**Code**
8	Home Canning of Fruits and Vegetables	122E
10	Home Freezing of Fruits and Vegetables	123E
56	How to Make Jellies, Jams and Preserves at Home	124E
74	Food and Your Weight	031E
119	Storing Vegetables and Fruits in Basements, Cellars, Out-buildings and Pits	028E
208	Soybeans in Family Meals	027E
217	Drying Foods at Home	117E
	Sweeteners: Using and Storing Honey	545E
	Seasoning with Herbs and Spices	544E
	Can Your Kitchen Pass the Food Storage Test	541E
	Safe Use of Microwave Ovens	577E
	Growing Vegetables in the Home Garden	110E
	Mini Gardens for Vegetables	111E

10

Nutrition Powers the Family

Regardless of how healthy you are, understanding the basics of nutrition and applying that knowledge can help you and your family live life to its full potential. You cannot manage time, train your children, handle money wisely, or reach out to others if you cannot think clearly, if you feel tired and grouchy, and if you never seem to have much energy. Two-thirds of our calories today are supplied by foods from which the original nutrients are mostly or wholly discarded.

Many of us would like to go back to basics in cooking and find we do not know how. We grew up in the "lost skills generation" when women who had more money than time bought the many convenience foods that appeared in the market shortly after World War II.

We also face the confusion of conflicting ideas given by leading nutritionists. One expert warns that preservatives may cause cancer, and another dismisses such warnings as silly and unfounded. We take stewardship of our bodies seriously. We want to be informed and knowledgeable, but what is right?

Fortunately, we have been making strides in the right direction. We consume less whole milk, cream, butter, eggs, and animal fat—all foods that tend to raise blood cholesterol. We have increased our consumption of vegetable oils.

We favor foods naturally fortified with vitamins and minerals over those that use chemical additives and preservatives. Many shoppers read labels.

More and more people use honey, molasses, and the less refined sugars rather than highly processed white sugar. There is a trend toward the whole grain flours and baked goods and away from the use of white flour and fluffy white bread.

Large chain supermarkets are installing natural food sections for shoppers looking for protein from seeds, nuts, and legumes such as soybeans, lentils, and split peas in addition to high-priced meat.

Hearty cereals such as granola and whole grains such as brown rice, millet, and wheat berries are beginning to catch on. People have become aware of the value of foods high in dietary fiber such as whole grains, apples, and celery.

More and more people avoid empty calorie snacks. Instead, they eat fruits, nutritious food bars, or yogurt. Schools are beginning to appreciate the value of nutritious snacks.

Many people have quit smoking, although unfortunately a large number of youngsters have taken up the habit. People exercise more and consciously try to stay physically fit. A remarkable decrease in heart disease reflects our improved life-style, but we can do much more to insure good health for ourselves and our families.

It may not be as simple as it sounds. No matter how informed you are, you may find it very, very difficult to change your eating habits. For many reasons, people resist change in how and what they eat.

Kathie is an enthusiastic person. When she got caught up in the nutritional revolution of the sixties, she became excited about the things she was learning. She drove across the city to buy whole wheat flour to make bread. She imagined how thrilled her family would be about her homemade bread and its nutritional value.

"I turned out bread as sweet as cake from my first bread recipe," Kathie recalls. "It had so much flavor we couldn't tell what kind of filling was in our sandwiches. As time passed my bread improved, and I felt a sense of deep satisfaction as I watched the girls leave for school carrying their lunch bags filled with nutritious food. Later I learned they had been trading off their lunches for chips and white bread!"

Dave was no more enthusiastic than Belinda and Stacy. One day after Kathie had added "a tiny little bit" of wheat germ to Dave's favorite meatloaf, he said, "Hey, Babe! Remember, we are your family, not the enemy!"

If you are the only one in the family interested in nutrition, go slowly and introduce nutritious supplements as unobtrusively as possible. This will be easier for the cook to accomplish than for others in the family.

Patience is important. Whole wheat, for example, has a lot of roughage. Your digestive system needs time to adapt to the dietary change. Get accustomed to wheat by using whole wheat flour a little at a time in your family's favorite recipes that call for white flour. Use this method in baking for a few weeks and gradually work up to one half whole wheat flour. Allow several more weeks to pass before increasing it.

Use cooked grains for breakfast only one or two times a week. Then slowly add wheat-related recipes to your daily diet.

One family became overeager to introduce all whole wheat into their diet. After two weeks of experimenting with many grain recipes, they began having severe abdominal pain and gas problems. Because they had been on a soft diet for years, their bodies reacted in shock to the sudden abundance of natural foods. Their doctor told them such an abrupt change of diet could cause intestinal bleeding, if continued. Once their bodies had adapted to the natural grains, they could eat them regularly and experience the good health resulting from the vitamins, minerals, and roughage in their natural state.

Do not talk nutrition endlessly. That will turn your family off quicker than anything else you can do. People awakened to nutrition are like new Christians, constantly excited by new insights. They like nothing better than to share them with others. Resist the temptation. A quiet, unobtrusive approach will pay off in the long run. Gradually, your family will get used to the change of diet. They may even appreciate and like it.

When this happens, your family will find vast new areas to explore together. Programs like Project F, sponsored by the United States government, provide opportunities to learn new skills. Families who have attended these classes in churches or schools have had a chance to see films such as *Diet for a Small Planet,* to learn how to make yogurt and sprout seeds, and to see wheat berries ground into flour.

Many did not know what a wheat berry was. They took home samples of these whole wheat kernels so that they could experiment and cook simple foods with them. The success they had generated so much enthusiasm that they wanted to go out and buy their own wheat right away.

You will meet new friends who will be glad to have you tell of your discoveries. These friends will also team up with you to split foods you want to buy in bulk. For example, noninstant powdered milk is generally sold by dairies in fifty-pound packages. If this is too much for you, you can split it with a friend or friends. You and a friend may want to split the cost of purchasing a stone mill to grind wheat if it is too expensive for each of you to buy individually. It is great fun to spend a morning baking bread with a friend. An experienced friend can help the beginner learn how to make bread without fear of failure.

Going back to basics will do far more for you than improve your health. It will help expand your mind and interests. It will save you money and time. It will increase your confidence and sense of well-being. You will feel in harmony with God and nature.

WHAT YOU NEED TO KNOW ABOUT FOODS

When planning balanced meals, think in terms of the basic food groups.

- Group 1: Milk, cheese, cottage cheese, yogurt, butter (mixed with safflower oil), buttermilk
- Group 2: Fresh meat, fish and poultry, peas, eggs, dry beans, nuts, and peanut butter
- Group 3: Dark green vegetables, balanced with yellow vegetables, citrus fruits, and tomatoes; vegetables eaten raw if possible; dried fruits
- Group 4: Whole-grain breads, cereals, enriched pasta (noodles), brown rice, wild rice, and seeds

For better nutrition, also consider—

- Sugars: Raw, uncooked, unfiltered honey and molasses
- Snacks: Raw vegetables, popcorn, nuts, dried fruit leather, baked goods with whole grains, yogurt sweetened with pineapple or orange juice, sunflower seeds, baked custards, rice puddings, meat.

WHAT YOU SHOULD KNOW ABOUT FRUITS AND VEGETABLES

American diets are low in dark green leafy vegetables. For salads use more romaine and spinach, and toss in some fresh parsley. Do not count on iceberg lettuce for nutrients, because it is mostly water. Use more broccoli. Raise mustard greens. Use more Swiss chard than spinach (recipes are interchangeable). Buy the darkest green vegetables you can find.

Wash off your greens when you bring them home. Dip them up and down in cool water. Place them in your dish drainer in the sink for the excess water to run off. Then lay the greens on tea towels, which you roll up. Pat dry. Place the dry greens in plastic bags with paper towels in the bottom.

Fresh vegetables should be your first choice. Vegetables that are frozen immediately after picking also retain most of their nutrients. A fairly reliable rule of thumb: first, raw; second, frozen; third, canned (least desirable). The best way to retain vitamins during cooking is to steam the vegetables. Use one of the petal steamers that fit any size saucepan.

You can interchange fruits and vegetables in your diet as long as you get four daily. That may be one fruit and three vegetables or two fruits and two vegetables, and so on.

GENERAL GUIDELINES FOR IMPROVING EATING HABITS

Cut down on red meats, sugar, salt, white flour.

Eat more whole grains, fresh vegetables and fruits, fish and poultry.

Increase protein intake at breakfast. To increase and prolong energy when you need it most, make breakfast your high-protein meal.

Try new foods. Take advantage of the variety of food available to you. Be creative when cooking, using as much of the whole food as possible. Try eating a different vegetable each week and look for new ways to use food you may normally throw away, like carrot tops or the seeds from the winter squashes.

Use cooked whole-grain cereals.

Make your own bread.

Learn to use mixed grains to increase the usable protein in your diet. Grains: wheat, oats, barley, rye, rice, corn, millet (cook millet as cream of wheat): Legumes: beans, lentils, split peas, peanuts.

Use polyunsaturated oils. These oils have a natural balance, having saturated fats in them also, but polyunsaturated fatty acids are in larger amounts.

Be a careful label-reader when it comes to margarine. The first ingredient listed is the clue. If the label says hydrogenated or hardened oil, then the product is mostly saturated oil. If you find a brand you like, make your own diet margarine by whipping ice water into it.

Butter should be U.S. Grade AA and made from sweet cream (salt it yourself). Make your own unsaturated butter, which is nutritionally superior and better tasting. Let a pound of butter (2 cups) warm to room temperature. Place in a big bowl and whip (electric mixer) three to five minutes. Slowly add one cup safflower oil (up to 1½ cups). Salt it. You can add honey to a portion of it to make honey butter.

Milk: Make your own yogurt and buttermilk. Use noninstant

nonfat dried milk. (Not for babies unless your doctor says a nonfat dried milk should be used). Make custards, rice puddings, peanut butter treats.

MAKE SNACK FOODS COUNT

Most of us grew up with the teaching that we should not eat between meals. Now some researchers suggest that five or six small meals a day will keep us healthier than eating one or two big meals.

Children need fewer calories than adults, but everything they eat should be nutritious. Many children require between-meal snacks because they do not eat enough at mealtimes to supply the energy they need.

Help your family get needed nutrients by keeping two trays of snacks stocked and easy to find. Keep one in the refrigerator and the other on a kitchen shelf.

On the refrigerator tray put cheese cubes, cold meat, fruit, celery sticks filled with cream cheese or peanut butter, carrots, cucumber or green pepper slices, baked custard, yogurt. Encourage your children to drink milk with their snacks.

On the shelf tray include dried fruit and raisins, fruit leather, nuts, sunflower seeds, popcorn, granola cereal or trail-mix, whole grain snack bars, graham crackers, oatmeal cookies made with whole wheat flour, peanut butter on crackers.

Begin with a wide assortment of finger foods. Keep track of what has to be replaced most often. Vary the snacks in line with seasonal variations, but also keep popular items on hand.

Encourage children to make their own snacks, too. Here is a recipe that is fun as well as tasty.

Peanut Butter Candy (1)

Mix 1 cup crunchy peanut butter with 1 cup honey
Slowly add 1½ to 2 cups dried nonfat milk
Make into walnut-sized balls and roll in almonds, seeds coconut, nuts, or granola. Chill.

Peanut Butter Candy (2)

Mix 2 cups peanut butter with 1 cup chopped cooked prunes
Add ¼ cup nonfat dried milk
When "play dough" texture, roll in homemade granola.
Chill balls. Makes about 30.

Does your child like Jello, which is eighty-five percent sugar?
As an option make a fruited dessert by using unflavored gelatin.
Bring 1½ cups apple or orange juice to boil. Sprinkle 1 package of
gelatin over ¼ cup fruit juice or water. Stir hot and cold mixtures
together and add 1 cup fruit, when partially set.

Establish a regular snack time so the children will not be eating
continually or too close to mealtime. By supplying nutritious
snacks you can break them of the habit of eating sweets and other
foods with empty calories and help supply some of the vitamins,
minerals, and protein they may have missed at mealtime.

WHEAT AND OTHER GRAINS DESERVE SPECIAL ATTENTION

"Give us this day our daily bread" (Matthew 6:11).

NUTRITIONAL IMPORTANCE OF GRAINS

Since the days of early man, grains have been important to
good health. Commonly used whole grains include wheat, rye,
corn, unpearled barley, oats, millet, buckwheat, and whole-grain
brown rice. These grains are an important dietary source of proteins, fats, and carbohydrates. They offer a good complement of
several vitamins. Among the most important are vitamins B_1, B_3
(niacin), B_6, folic acid, and vitamin E. Iron and zinc are among
the important minerals in whole grains.

The usable protein in food depends on the presence of amino
acids. If all eight of the essential amino acids are present, the
food is a *complete protein*. Protein in grains is not complete, but
with the addition of animal protein such as milk, meat, or cheese,
or different vegetable proteins such as legumes, nuts, or seeds,
we can get complete proteins by what is known as *combining*

By combining certain incomplete plant sources, a protein that is lacking in one essential amino acid can be eaten with a protein that has a large amount of the missing amino acid, thereby completing the structure of the eight essential amino acids.

To improve the usability of incomplete proteins, add a small amount of complete proteins such as eggs, milk, and cheese at the same meal. Examples of this would be macaroni and cheese, buritos (wheat and beans), rice pudding (rice and milk), chili and cornbread, tacos (corn and beans), Oriental foods, peanut butter on whole wheat bread.

Although meat is high in the amino acid lysine, it is low in the essential amino acid methionine. Wheat is high in methionine, but low in lysine. Meat and bread actually complement each other.

We usually think of meat as the chief supplier of protein. Cereals and grains are also very high in this nutrient and can be produced far more economically than meat.

Frances Moore Lappe in *Diet for a Small Planet* says: "An acre of cereal grains can produce five times more protein than an acre devoted to meat production. Legumes (peas, beans, lentils) can produce 10 times more, leafy vegetables can produce 15 times more and spinach 26 times more protein per acre than beef."[1]

We lose much of the value of grains through refining. Nature has packed nutrients into wheat, for example. The whole kernel's interior, or endosperm, contains starch and a protein called gluten. The body needs the vitamins and minerals found in the germ before it can use the starch and protein to produce energy and repair tissues.

Unfortunately, all these vitamins and minerals are lost in refining. Also lost from the wheat germ by refining is the amino acid lysine. This loss causes a severe imbalance in the protein. The hull of the wheat, also removed in processing, contains valuable fiber. Preliminary studies at Loma Linda University show that fiber in food in a *natural* state lowers serum cholesterol.

A KERNEL

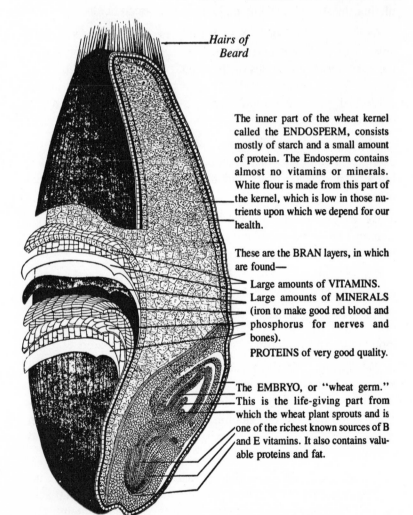

Hairs of Beard

The inner part of the wheat kernel called the ENDOSPERM, consists mostly of starch and a small amount of protein. The Endosperm contains almost no vitamins or minerals. White flour is made from this part of the kernel, which is low in those nutrients upon which we depend for our health.

These are the BRAN layers, in which are found—

Large amounts of VITAMINS.
Large amounts of MINERALS (iron to make good red blood and phosphorus for nerves and bones).
PROTEINS of very good quality.

The EMBRYO, or "wheat germ." This is the life-giving part from which the wheat plant sprouts and is one of the richest known sources of B and E vitamins. It also contains valuable proteins and fat.

Longitudinal Section of a Grain of Wheat

OF WHEAT

SELECTED HIGH PROTEIN WHEAT USED BY EL MOLINO MILLS CONTAINS THESE ESSENTIAL MINERALS AND VITAMINS:

MINERALS

Calcium	Iodine
Iron	Fluorine
Phosphorus	Chlorine
Magnesium	Sodium
Potassium	Silicon
Manganese	Boron
Copper	Barium
Sulphur	Silver

And Other Trace Minerals

VITAMINS:

Thiamine B-1
Riboflavin B-2 or G
Niacin
Pantothenic Acid
Pyridoxine B-6
Biotin or H
Inositol
Folic Acid
Choline
Vitamin E

Plus at least four other vitamin factors generally found in Bran and Wheat Germ.

In white flour about one-half of the fat is lost. This fat has a high food value, since it contains unsaturated fatty acids and vitamin B₁, all of which are nutritionally very important.

Ask for Whole Grain Flour and Cereals
at Your Nearest Dietary Food Store.

Compliments of El Molino Mills City of Industry, California.

We can clearly see that we need to eat the whole wheat berry to receive the natural proportion of food value from the grain. Once the kernel is cracked or ground into flour, the high quality protein, vitamins, and minerals become active. The wheat germ, considered one of the highest natural sources of the B vitamins and of vitamin E, is considerably reduced through oxidation within seventy-two hours after grinding unless it is kept in an airtight container.

By learning to grind your own wheat berries you retain the most nutrients by cracking or grinding only as many wheat berries as you need. Store unused cracked or ground wheat in the refrigerator or freezer to prevent loss of nutrients.

Some people would rather go to a natural foods store and buy small amounts of cracked and ground wheat and not bother grinding it themselves. A flour mill or grinder, however, is useful in many different ways. It will grind flour or meal, and it will powder all grains, seeds, nuts, herbs, even dry mushrooms.

BASIC TOOLS AVAILABLE FOR GRINDING

Hand grinder. A hand grinder, available with metal buhr, takes a lot of muscle power, but many families use them. They are good for cracked wheat, but cannot grind the flour fine enough to produce *light* loaves of bread.

Electric blender. Many of us have electric blenders that are designed to chop, mix, and so on. These also work well for cracking grain. If you have enough patience to grind grain into flour one cup at a time, try it. To avoid overheating your blender, let it rest periodically.

Electric stone mill. For a *light* loaf of bread, it is best to grind wheat berries in a large mill. These mills are designed to crack or grind grains of all kinds. If you make all your own bread, the mill will pay for itself by the end of the first year.

BREAD MAKING APPLIANCES

Standard electric mixers. These can be used for the beginning stages of bread making.

Heavy duty electric mixers. These electric mixers have dough hooks for mixing and kneading. They are convenient and save time for families who make all their own bread. Most mixers come with a separate bowl and wire whips for making cakes, frostings, and so on.

EXPERIMENTING WITH GRAINS

You can discover hundreds of tasty ways to include grains in your diet. If you do not have the interest or time to develop your own recipes, you will find many excellent books to help. One of the best is *The El Molino Cookbook,* published by El Molino Mills.

We have developed the recipes in this book to expose you to the many ways wheat can be used in the daily diet. Both beginning and experienced cooks will enjoy trying these ideas.

If you are working with a group of people who would like to experiment with grains, the least expensive way to do this is to buy 100 pounds of wheat and split it into 10-pound packages. This will cost each person $1.40 to $1.80 (depending on source) for 10 pounds of wheat.

Wheat berries can be used as cereal or tossed into soups and salads. Cracked wheat, served as hot cereal, was the mainstay of the early American diet. Serve it with one-half cup of milk to increase the usable protein. Cracked wheat is also an alternative to rice dishes such as pilaf and can be used as a meat extender as well.

RECIPES

Whole Wheat Berries (serves 4 to 6)

1 cup wheat (makes 3 cups cooked wheat)
¼ to ½ tsp. salt (to taste)
2 cups water

Cooking method 1: Place wheat and water in covered pan or casserole in a 150° to 200° oven overnight. Ready to eat in the morning.

Cooking method 2: In top of double boiler, bring water to boil over direct heat. Slowly add wheat and stir. Cover and place pan on bottom of double boiler in which water is simmering. Cook at

204 The Complete Book of Home Management

least 3 hours until grains burst open and become soft.

If you have never before eaten whole wheat as a hot breakfast cereal, try this experiment with your family. Place one-fourth to one-half cup of cereal in each custard cup. Try plain, with butter, sugar or honey, cinnamon and raisins, cashews or other nuts. Let everyone pick his favorite. Each person should include one-half cup of milk with this meal to increase protein usability.

> • President Coolidge's favorite breakfast was one part rye to two parts of wheat cooked the double boiler method. He then added sugar and milk.
>
> • New research has found that adding rye to wheat, cooked either method, will complete the essential amino acids group. This is a good source of vitamin B, phosphorus, iron, calcium, potassium, and vitamin D.

Cracked Wheat

1 cup wheat
¼ to ½ tsp. salt (to taste)
2 cups water

Crack wheat berries in mill on "coarse," or in electric blender. Sift out loose fine flour and store in refrigerator.

Cooking method 1: Slowly add wheat to boiling water and stir. Cover and cook on low for 30 minutes. (Some wheat takes 35 to 45 minutes)

Cooking method 2: In top of double boiler bring water to boil over direct heat. Slowly add wheat and stir. Cover and place pan on bottom of double boiler in which water is simmering. Cook 45 minutes to 1 hour.

For cereal, flavor to taste as for whole wheat berry cereal.

Note: Some grains require a little longer cooking time. Make adjustments in the amount of water if you need to.

Cooked Cracked and Whole Wheat Berries

Save leftover cooked wheat and store in a covered jar in the refrigerator. It will stay fresh for about one week. You can use the leftovers in many ways. Enjoy a quick breakfast by adding a little water and reheating. Toss some rich nuggets into your dinner soup. Mix one-half cup in your Waldorf and other fruit salads. Your family will love it! Leftover cracked and whole wheat berries are also good meat extenders when added to sauces, meatloaves, and most hamburger recipes.

Carrot-Pineapple Salad

Shred 1½ cups carrots. Add to ½ cup drained crushed pineapple. Mix in 1 cup cooked cracked wheat. Moisten with mayonnaise that has a little pineapple juice added to it. Salt to taste and chill. For a big salad for church, replace half the water with pineapple juice when cooking wheat. A sought-after recipe!

Golden Carrot-Raisin Salad

Toss 1½ cups shredded carrots, ½ cup seedless raisins, 1½ cups small pieces of orange, and 1 cup cooked cracked wheat. Moisten with mayonnaise and sprinkle with ½ cup chopped peanuts. A protein combination dish that tastes great!

Wheat Pilaf

This is one of the Lidens' ten main dinner recipes. It is a family favorite, and friends love it, too. Cracked wheat can be used as a main dish with nuts to increase the protein usage or as an alternate for many rice recipes.
1. As the main dish:
    2 T. butter
    2 T. green pepper, chopped
    ½ c. celery, chopped
    4 green onions, sliced fine
    ½ c. sliced almonds (or slivered)
    ⅛ tsp. marjoram (small leaves)

    ¼ tsp. oregano (small leaves)
    2 c. boiling water

2 chicken bouillon cubes
1 cup cracked (uncooked) wheat
  (sift out flour after cracking)
Salt to taste after cooking

In medium skillet sauté vegetables in butter until tender-crisp. In a two-quart saucepan dissolve bouillon cubes in boiling water. Slowly stir in cracked wheat. Immediately add vegetables, cover. Reduce heat to low and simmer thirty minutes. You may let it stand about ten minutes, fluff, and garnish with chopped green onion. Serve with green salad, Italian dressing, and fresh fruit.

2. As a side dish:
   2 T. butter
   2 T. green pepper, chopped
   ½ c. celery, chopped
   1 medium onion, chopped

   2 c. boiling water
   2 chicken bouillon cubes
   1 c. cracked wheat (sift out flour)

Follow directions for main dish. A simple way to change the flavor is to stir in (sauté stage) one or more of the following:
Almonds: ½ cup, slivered
Garlic: 1 mashed clove, chopped fine
Mushrooms: 1 can (3 or 4 oz.) sliced, or stems and pieces,
           drained.
Olives: ½ cup, chopped ripe
Parsley: 2 T., snipped

Meatballs

Cracked wheat is a great meat extender. You can fix these meatballs (master mix) for your family, or use the whole recipe and feed twenty people, with 1½ pounds of hamburger. You save lots of money and build health by raising the usable protein with a wheat and meat combination. Use leftover cooked grains if you wish. Mix until you think you have the texture to hold meatballs together. Amounts can vary depending on your wishes. Or toss cooked wheat into the crumbly hamburger that you are frying to make regular meat sauce for spaghetti. Ground cooked soybeans mixed with hamburger makes a good meat sauce, too.

3 c. cracked wheat (uncooked)
1½ lbs. lean hamburger
2 beaten eggs
1 tsp. garlic.salt
1 tsp. oregano
¼ tsp. pepper
3 T. chopped fresh parsley

Variations:
Add ½ cup Parmesan cheese and/or
¼ cup green pepper, finely chopped.
Replace garlic salt with 1 minced
clove of garlic.

Make into small balls. Either drop balls into sauce to cook, or first brown 10 minutes on each side in a 350° oven. Cook in sauce 40 minutes to 1½ hours. Cooked grains make about 100 balls, uncooked grains make 60 to 80 balls.

Note for dieters: Steam fresh bean sprouts instead of noodles.

BREAD MAKING MADE EASY

Making bread need not be a complicated, scary project. It can be very simple and failure-proof if you follow some basic rules. Many of us gained confidence as beginners by working with a friend. Whether alone or with a friend, practice makes perfect, and each loaf of bread you turn out will give you more confidence and courage.

Compare learning to make bread to experiencing a new baby in the family. Everything throughout the day revolves around the baby. By the time you have two or three children, things change. The children fit into *your* schedule, and things seem to adjust and take care of themselves. By the time you have made bread three or four times, bread making also blends into your schedule and can become a part of your normal routine.

Warm, sunny days are ideal for making bread. A warm kitchen will help your dough rise faster. Rain or shine, once you get enthusiastic about bread making, every day is the perfect day. But in a cool kitchen the dough will take longer to rise.

Active dry yeast comes in granules and is very easy to work with. Since yeast feeds on sugar, dissolve about one tablespoon of brown sugar in warm water before sprinkling yeast over the water. Do not stir. The water temperature must be between 105° and 115° to develop the yeast. A candy thermometer will work nicely to guide you to the right temperature. Or check the temperature by putting a little water on your wrist just like checking the temperature of a baby's bottle. If the water temperature is too cool, the yeast will be sluggish. If it is too hot, it will kill the yeast growth.

Use polyunsaturated oils such as safflower oil. Try honey instead of sugar to activate yeast. Measure the oil first, then measure the honey, and it will slide out of the cup. Salt slows down the action of yeast so add salt after your yeast mixture has bubbled. If your recipe calls for eggs, beat them and use them as part of the liquid to add protein and richness, and produce a lighter bread.

Everyone has his own favorite type of bread. Some people like light-colored, feathery bread, and others like dense, darker bread. If you are a beginner at bread making, avoid—temporarily—adding rye, wheat germ, buckwheat, cornmeal, powdered milk, and other low-gluten products until you have made beautiful, high loaves of bread and have the "feel" of good dough.

Flour contains a protein substance called *gluten*. Bread recipes seldom state an *exact* amount of flour, beating, kneading, and rising time because flours are not exactly the same in their gluten content. The gluten is activated when the flour is moistened, mixed, and kneaded. After you have added flour to the liquid mixture and have beaten it four or five minutes you can see the gluten developing as the batter becomes glossy and elastic.

Methods of bread making make a difference. You can take two

people, give them the same ingredients, and the person who makes the bread by hand will usually have a smaller (but just as tasty) loaf of bread. When you make bread by hand you cannot whip as much air into the batter, and in the kneading process you usually have to add extra flour so the dough does not stick to your hands. An electric mixer has the power to whip in extra air and build gluten without adding extra flour.

Here is a recipe created by Kathie for the bewildered beginning bread baker.

Honey Wheat Bread (2 loaves)

This bread can be made by hand or with electric mixer (3 to 4 qt. bowl). You will need two metal pans 9-by-5 inches (8-by-4, in a pinch). You will also need about seven cups of freshly ground whole wheat flour. Ask the merchant at your natural foods store to grind it fresh for full flavor.

As you read the recipe, do not get nervous when you notice it calls for three cups of flour "plus or minus." As you follow the instructions you will be able to feel what is right.

Rising time depends on the amount of gluten in the flour and on the temperature. It could take twenty minutes or up to an hour for the dough to rise.

Ingredients, step 1:

       1 tablespoon brown sugar
       1 cup warm water (110°)
       1 package (about 2 T.) active dry yeast

Ingredients, step 2:

       1¾ cup warm water
       ¼ cup oil
       ½ cup honey
       1 beaten egg
       1 tablespoon salt
       3½ cups whole wheat flour

Ingredients, step 3:
>   1 cup flour (white)
>   3 cups whole wheat flour (plus or minus)

Note: Mixing by hand will require one-half to one cup white flour (extra) for board, hands, and kneading

Method, step 1:
>   Dissolve brown sugar in warm water (110°) and sprinkle yeast on top. Should bubble in 5 to 10 minutes.

Method, step 2:
>   Add 1¾ cups warm water, oil, honey, beaten egg, and salt. Stir in, 1 cup at a time, 3½ cups whole wheat flour. Beat by hand 300 strokes, or with mixer on low, 4 to 5 minutes.

Method, step 3:
>   *By hand.* Stir in 1 cup white flour and as much whole wheat flour as you can handle, until dough leaves side of bowl. On floured board make a cushion of remaining whole wheat flour. Turn dough out onto cushion, cover with light coating of flour and towel. Let rest 10 minutes. Begin kneading and keep a light coat of flour on dough. Takes about 10 minutes to become smooth and elastic. Add as little extra flour as possible to keep a light loaf of bread.

>   *By electric mixer.* With dough hook in place, add 1 cup white flour and 3 cups whole wheat flour. Knead on low 10 minutes.

Method, step 4:
>   Place in oiled bowl and cover. Let rise in warm place to just under doubled. Grease pans with shortening. Oil breadboard and hands. Punch dough down and cut into two loaves. Cover and let rest 10 minutes. Shape into loaves. Fill pans 2/3 full, brush tops with oil, cover and let rise 1/3, or just under double. Preheat oven 10 minutes (important to bread). Bake at 375° for 40 to 45 minutes.

Method, step 5:
Test for doneness (tap for hollow sound). Cool on racks. For soft crust, brush with butter and cover with towel.

Method, step 6:
Eat, and praise the Lord!

You do not have to become a food faddist to give nutrition high priority in your marriage. What good nutrition really boils down to is getting back to basics: eating a well-balanced diet, which consists of a wide variety of foods including fish and vegetables, meats poultry, whole grains, and dairy products; and cutting down on red meat, white sugar, white flour, and salt. Moderation is the key.

Notes

CHAPTER 1

1. Janet Chan, "Old Age: You Are What You Were," *McCall's* 103 (November 1975): 40.
2. Edwin Diamond, "Clues to Being More Successful," *Reader's Digest,* May 1975, pp. 88-91.

CHAPTER 5

1. Dee Engel, "Redeem the Time," *Perspective,* Winter 1977, pp. 7-9.

CHAPTER 7

1. Grace W. Weinstein, *Children and Money* (New York: Charterhouse, 1975), pp. 124-25.

CHAPTER 8

1. Richard Morse, "A Five-year Plan for Managing Your Money," *Changing Times,* October 1973, p. 46.

CHAPTER 9

1. Beatrice Hunter, *Natural Foods Primer* (New York: Simon and Schuster, 1972), p. 126.

CHAPTER 10

1. Frances Moore Lappe, *Diet for a Small Planet* (New York: Ballentine, 1972), p. 13.

Selected Bibliography

Allen, Evanthia. "Free up Your Time." *Good Ideas for Decorating,* Fall 1977, p. 33.

Alter, Jo Anna. "A Guide to Organizing Your Time—And Saving It Too!" *Family Circle,* November 1976, p. 42.

Ashton, Marvin J. *One for the Money.* Salt Lake City: Deseret, 1975.

Baer, Jean. "Do You Have Too Much to Do?" *Woman's Day,* May 1976, p. 74.

Berry, Jo. *The Happy Home Handbook.* Old Tappan, N.J.: Revell, 1976.

Bird, Caroline, and Ashby, Babeet. "Do Working Wives Have Better Marriages?" *Family Circle,* November 1976, p. 58.

Bliss, Edwin C. *Getting Things Done.* New York: Scribner's, 1976.

———. "The Time of Your Life: How to Use It, Stretch It, Save It." *House & Garden,* August 1976, p. 42.

Brandt, Henry, and Landrum, Phil. *I Want to Enjoy My Children.* Grand Rapids: Zondervan, 1975.

Bunner, Sandra. *Foods, Preparation, Storage, and You.* Sacramento: Calico West, 1972.

Burgess, Constance. *Be a Better Buyer.* Berkeley, Calif.: U. of California, September 1971.

Carlson, Dwight L. *Run and Not Be Weary.* Old Tappan, N.J.: Revell, 1974.

Carper, Jean. "Consumer Watch, Labels and The Law." *American Home,* January 1978, p. 12.

Cazalas, James K. "Mini Maids Attack Dust and Grime." *The Sacramento Union,* 14 March 1976.

Clineball, Charlotte Holt. *Meet Me in the Middle.* New York: Harper & Row, 1973.

The Complete Family Sewing Book. New York: Curtin, 1972.

Cook, Louise. "Learning How to Shop and Save." *Sacramento Bee,* 5 September 1977.

Cooking with Gourmet Grains. Seattle: Stone-Buhr Milling, 1971.

Craig, Betty. "Organizing Your Time." *Woman's World,* June 1977, p. 12.

Crenshaw, Mary Ann. "High Vitality Drinks from High-Energy People." *Family Circle,* November 1977, p. 93.

Crocker, Betty. *Starting Out.* New York: Golden, 1975.

Curtin, Barbara. "Kindergartners Discover Healthy Foods Can Be Tasty." *The Oregonian,* 18 January 1978.

David, Lester. "How to Stretch Your Inflated Money." *Reader's Digest,* February 1970, p. 61.

Davis, Adelle. *Let's Eat Right To Keep Fit.* New York: Harcourt Brace Jovanovich, 1970.

Davis, Flora. "How 85,000 Women Feel About Food and Cooking." *Redbook Magazine,* January 1975, p. 10.

Donnelly, Caroline. "How Hard Should You Work?" *Reader's Digest,* August 1975, p. 145.

Eckles, Robert W.; Carmichael, Ronald L.; and Sarchet, Bernard R. *Essentials of Management for First-Line Supervision.* New York: Wiley, 1974.

Eicholz, Jack. "Hassle over Homework." *Home Life,* March 1977, p. 34.

Eisen, Carol G. *Nobody Said You Had to Eat off the Floor.* New York: McKay, 1971.

The El Molino Cookbook. City of Industry, Calif.: El Molino Mills, 1976.

Emerson, Gloria. "How Rose Kennedy Survived." *McCall's,* August 1975, p. 68.

215

Engstrom, Ted W., and Dayton, Edward R. *The Art of Management for Christian Leaders*. Waco, Tex.: Word, 1976.

Evilsizer, Marion. "The Family Bookkeeper." *Woman's Day,* April 1973.

————. *Family Fare*. Home & Garden Bulletin No. 1. Rev. ed. Washington, D.C.: U.S. Dept. of Agriculture, 1974.

Fitzpatrick, Nancy. "Shopping Secrets from a Professional Bargain Hunter." *Family Circle,* March 1976, p. 18.

Fleming, Alice. "Putting Housework in Its Place." *Woman's Day,* February 1977, p. 12.

"For the Home." *The Sacramento Union,* 16 June 1976.

"Furnishing a Home? Plan Before You Spend." *Good Ideas for Decorating,* Fall 1977, p. 48.

Galloway, Dale E. *Dream a New Dream*. Wheaton, Ill.: Tyndale, 1975.

————. "Success Born Out of Failures." Sermon #528. Mimeographed. Portland, Ore.: New Hope Community Church, n.d.

Gibson, Gwen. "Happy Rockefeller: An Old-fashioned Mom Who Rules With Love." *Family Weekly,* 9 May 1976, p. 4.

Gilbreth, Lillian M.; Thomas, Orpha Mae; and Clymer, Eleanor. *Management in the Home*. New York: Dodd, Mead, 1959.

Gittelson, Natalie. "How Women Feel About Housework." *McCall's,* February 1977, p. 129.

Goldbeck, Nikki, and Goldbeck, David. *The Supermarket Handbook*. New York: New Amer. Lib., 1976.

Goldfein, Donna. *Every Woman's Guide to Time Management*. Milbrae, Calif.: Les Femmes, 1977.

Goodman, Ellen. "Teaching Children About Money." *Family Circle,* March 1976, p. 80.

Graubard, Paul S. "How I Stopped Nagging and Started Teaching My Children to Behave." *McCall's,* May 1977, p. 90.

Greer, Rebecca. *How to Live Rich When You're Not*. New York: Grossett and Dunlap, 1977.

Gross, Paul H. "A Run for Your Money." *House & Garden,* August 1976, p. 42.

Hancock, Maxine. *Love, Honor & Be Free*. Chicago: Moody, 1975.

Harrell, Irene Burt. *Muddy Sneakers and Other Family Hassles*. Nashville: Abingdon, 1974.

Harris, Phyllis. "How to Earn Extra $$$." *Family Circle,* May 1975, p. 2.

Havemann, Ernest. "Marriage's Eight Money Traps." *Reader's Digest,* October 1971, p. 91.

Heilman, Joan Rattner. "How I Did It." *Great Ideas for Women Who Work,* March 1978, p. 80.

Hochstein, Rollie. "How to Get Ahead and Keep a Husband Happy." *Woman's Day,* October 1976, p. 60.

———. "Ideas for Living: No. 13." *Family Circle,* July 1974, p. 12.

———. "Ten Ways to Help Your Child Succeed." *Woman's Day,* 28 June 1977, p. 54.

Home Care of Purchased Frozen Foods. Home & Garden Bulletin No. 69. Washington, D.C.: U.S. Dept. of Agriculture, n.d.

Hoole, Daryl V. *The Art of Homemaking*. Salt Lake City: Deseret, 1967.

———. *The Joys of Homemaking*. Salt Lake City: Deseret, 1975.

Hooper, Doug. *You Are What You Think,* Nos. 1-3. Danville, Calif.: Hooper, 1975, 1976, 1977.

Horine, Don. "How To Improve Your Marriage." *National Enquirer,* 14 June 1977.

Horn, Marilyn J. *Carrying It Off in Style! The Role of Clothing*. Handbook for the Home. Washington, D.C.: U.S. Dept. of Agriculture, 1973.

How to Live on Your Income. Edited by *Reader's Digest* editors. New York: Norton, 1970.

Hummel, Charles E. *Tyranny of the Urgent*. Downers Grove, Ill.: InterVarsity, 1974.

Hunt, Morton, and Hunt, Bernice. "You're Not the Woman I Married!" *Great Ideas for Women Who Work,* March 1978, p. 68.

Hyde, Vance. *And Everything Nice*. New York: McKay, 1959.

217

Kelly, Marguerite, and Parsons, Elia. *The Mother's Almanac.* Garden City, N.Y.: Doubleday, 1975.

Kiev, Ari. *A Strategy for Daily Living.* New York: Free, 1973.

———. *A Strategy for Success.* New York: Macmillan, 1977.

King, Janet Spencer. "Get Smart." *American Home,* May 1977, p. 38.

Laird, Jean E. "Increasing Your Energy." *Weight Watchers,* August 1974, p. 34.

Lakein, Alan. *How to Get Control of Your Time and Your Life.* New York: New Amer. Lib., 1973.

———. "How Organized Are You—REALLY?" *House & Garden,* August 1976, p. 43.

———. "How to Organize Your Household to Give You Time for All the Things You Want to Do." *House & Garden,* August 1973, p. 54.

Lappe, Frances Moore. *Diet for a Small Planet.* New York: Ballantine, 1972.

Lindborg, Peter. "Family Money Management." *Better Homes and Gardens,* December 1968, p. 8.

Lobsenz, Norman M. "How Husbands Really Feel about Working Wives." *Woman's Day,* July 1976, p. 8.

———. "Yours-Mine-Ours." *Woman's Day,* November 1976, p. 90.

Lobsenz, Norman M., and Laswell, Marcia. "Is There Any Time Left for Each Other?" *Family Weekly,* 7 November 1976, p. 12.

———. *No-Fault Marriage.* Garden City, N.Y.: Doubleday, 1976.

Mace, David, and Mace, Vera. *We Can Have Better Marriages.* Nashville: Abingdon, 1974.

Mackenzie, R. Alec. "How to Make the Most of Your Time." *U.S. News and World Report,* 3 December 1973, p. 45.

"Marriages Need Love—And Preparation." *Signs of the Times,* August 1975, p. 7.

Mason, Jo. "I Feed a Family of Four on $30 a Week." *Family Circle,* November 1977, p. 30.

Matthews, Charles. "Is Your Family Emotionally Healthy and Happy?" *Family Circle,* February 1977, p. 56.

Mayer, Jean, and Dwyer, Johanna. "Norwegians Take Eating to Heart." *The Oregonian,* 15 September 1977.

Maynard, Fredelle, and Maynard, Rona. "It Can Be a Very Hard Thing to Do, But Sometimes You Simply Have to Say No." *Woman's Day,* May 1974, p. 40.

McGrady, Mike. *The Kitchen Sink Papers.* Garden City, N.Y.: Doubleday, 1975.

McLean, Keitha. "Streamlined Living and How to Do It." *American Home,* May 1976, p. 44.

Miller, Mary Susan. "Do Men and Women Expect the Same Things from Marriage?" *Family Weekly,* 8 May 1977, p.18.

Moore, Charles W. *Why Your Money Never Seems to Reach.* Anaheim, Calif.: Moore, 1958.

Moore, Raymond S. "Help at Home." *Signs of the Times,* September 1975, p. 15.

O'Brien, Robert. "How to Save Money: In the Clothing Store." *Reader's Digest,* April 1970, p. 65.

Oddo, Sandra. "Children—Does Your Household Revolve Too Much Around Your Children." *House & Garden,* July 1975, p. 59.

Omohundro, Delight Dixon. *How to Win the Grocery Game.* New York: Drake, 1973.

O'Neill, Nena, and O'Neill, George. "You Can Change Your Life." *Family Circle,* April 1974, p. 149.

O'Reilly, Jane. "How to Get Control of Your Time." *New York Magazine,* January 17, 1972.

Pascoe, Elizabeth Jean. "How to Organize Everything." *Woman's Day,* October 1976, p. 20.

———. "How Working Women Cope." *Woman's Day,* July 1977, p. 90.

Pearce, Carol. "Budgeting Your Time." *Weight Watchers,* October 1975, p. 4.

Phillips, Barty. *How to Decorate Your Home Without Going Broke.* Garden City, N.Y.: Doubleday, 1975.

Poppy, John. "How to Find Time for What You Really Want to Do." *McCall's,* August 1972, p. 71.

Porter, Sylvia. *Sylvia Porter's Money Book.* Garden City, N.Y.: Doubleday, 1975.

Potter, Cecil A. "What—Resolutions Again!" *Psychology for Living,* January 1975, p. 5.

Rice, Shirley. *The Christian Home.* Norfolk, Va.: Norfolk Christ. Sch., 1972.

Rodgers, Dorothy, and Rodgers, Mary. "Of Two Minds." *McCall's,* January 1976, p. 24.

Rubin, Theodore I. "Psychiatrist's Notebook." *Ladies' Home Journal,* February 1977, p. 54.

Rush, Anna Fisher, and Schierberl, Margaret. "Finding Storage Space You Didn't Know You Had." *McCall's,* March 1974, p. 88.

Russell, Beverly. "The Talk-It-Over Technique." *House & Garden,* June 1977, p. 30.

"School Lunches That Kids Really Love." *Parade,* 15 January 1978, p. 12.

Schuller, Robert H. *Move Ahead with Possibility Thinking.* Garden City, N.Y.: Doubleday, 1967.

Seebohm, Caroline. "The Organized Mind—An Interview with Gregory Bateson." *House & Garden,* August 1976, p. 40.

Shedd, Charlie W. *Talk to Me.* Garden City, N.Y.: Doubleday, 1975.

Skelsey, Alice. *Working Mother's Guide to Her Home, Her Family and Herself.* New York: Random House, 1970.

Somerville, Rose M. *Introduction to Family Life and Sex Education.* Englewood Cliffs, N.J.: Prentice Hall, 1972.

Stevenson, Gladys T., and Miller, Cora. *Introduction to Foods and Nutrition.* New York: Wiley, 1960.

Storing Vegetables and Fruits in Basements, Cellars, Outbuildings and Pits. Home & Garden Bulletin No. 119. Washington, D.C.: U.S. Dept. of Agriculture, 1973.

Sudweeks, Deanna Smith. *Kitchen Magic.* Pleasant Grove, Utah: Kitchen Magic, 1974.

Swell, Dr. Lila. "Chart Your Way to Success." *Woman's Day.* January 1977, p. 62.

"Teaching Your Child About Money." *Moneysworth, The Consumer Newsletter,* 14 April 1972.

Tyson, Robert. "How to Cut a Task Down to Your Size, Get It Done and on Time." *House & Garden,* September 1975, p. 28.

Valentry, Duane. "Eleven Ways to Harness Worry." *Weight Watchers,* January 1973, p. 32.

Van Derbur, Marilyn. "Defeat Doesn't Mean Failure." *Listen,* October 1975, p. 6.

Vegetables in Family Meals. Home & Garden Bulletin No. 105. Washington, D.C.: U.S. Dept. of Agriculture, 1975.

Viorst, Judith. "How I Work at Home—And Still Work." *Redbook Magazine,* January 1975, p. 33.

Wagner, Junia, and Nyheim, Charlotte. "Consumer Nutrition TV Valley Consortium for Community College Television." Mimeographed. Sacramento, Calif.: Community College Consortium, 1976.

Wagner, Maurice E. "Breaking Out of the Hurry-Hurry Trap." *Psychology for Living,* March 1975, p. 8.

Walt, Dorothy. "Investigate Before Buying." *Consumer Affairs,* 23 February 1973.

How to Plan a Wardrobe. Pamphlet. New York: Hearst, 1970.

Warren, Bonnie. *Grains Make Gains in Cereals.* Bel Air Food Guide Pamphlet. Sacramento, Calif.: Bel Air Markets, 1976.

Weinstein, Grace W. *Children and Money.* New York: Charterhouse, 1975.

Whyte, Karen Cross. *The Complete Sprouting Cookbook.* San Francisco: Troubador, 1973.

Wilhelm, Maria. "Ideas for Living No. 16." *Family Circle,* October 1975, p. 8.

Wille, Lois. "We Learned to Be Thrifty." *Family Circle,* March 1975, p. 2.

Wilson, Tom. *Promises to Myself.* Kansas City: Sheed & Ward, 1975.

Wright, H. Norman. *Communication: Key to Your Marriage.* Glendale, Calif.: Gospel Light, 1974.

Young, Amy Ross. *It Only Hurts Between Paydays.* Denver: Accent, 1967.

Zabriske, Bob R. *Family Storage Plan.* Salt Lake City: Book-craft, 1966.